MICROS(

2024

The Most Updated Crash Course from Beginner to Advanced Learn All the Functions and Features to Become a Pro in 7 Days or Less

James Holler

Table of Contents

Chapter 1. Introduction

Welcome to Microsoft Word 2024, an up-to-date tutorial that teaches you everything you need to know about Microsoft Word in order to stay current, confident, and productive. This book will teach you how to use MS Word's most helpful and remarkable features without stress. You'll learn how to create, edit, and format a document from the ground up like an expert, how to operate confidently and efficiently using MS Word's best shortcut commands, how to quickly insert and format photos, shapes, tables, and charts, and much more.

Microsoft Word, popularly called **MS-Word** or **Word,** is a word processing application developed by Microsoft Corporation. Word is part of Microsoft Office Suite and was launched in **1983**. It competed with WordPerfect (the most popular word processor then) to become the world-leading word processor since the **1990s** till date. The latest office suite is **Office 2021 and Office 365**. It can run on Windows, macOS, iOS, and Android operating systems.

The majority of essential Microsoft Word features have been around for a long time, and the fundamentals remain consistent across all editions. Keep reading if you have an older version of Word, Word 2021, or Word 365; this book will be very helpful to you.

MS Word allows you to create, edit, format, save, and print a wide range of professional-looking personal and business documents, including books, graphics, bills, resumes, reports, letters, photographs, emails, invites, catalogs, notes, certifications, newsletters, and more. It features a simple user interface and is very easy to use.

Getting Started

To start using MS word, you must have it installed on your computer or use it online. Some computers come with Microsoft Office preinstalled, but if you do not have it, you can get it following the steps below:

Buy MS Word

1. Open your web browser, e.g., Google Chrome.

2. Go to office website: www.office.com.

3. Click on **Get office** if you want an office or MS Word on your desktop and buy from the available options:

• **Office 365 Family** vs **Office 365 Personal**: Office 365 Family can be shared with up to six individuals, whilst Office 365 Personal can only be used by one person. They serve the same purpose and both demand ongoing subscriptions. For anyone who wants access to the most up-to-date office software and cloud services, Office 365 is the ideal alternative. It is compatible with Windows 11, 10, 8, 7, and Mac OS X.

• **Office Home & Student 2021**: This is the latest version of office available for a one-time payment and contains only the essential apps (Word, Excel, PowerPoint, Access, Outlook, OneNote, Team, and Publisher). You can only use it on Windows 11, 10, and macOS.

4. Install Microsoft Office, and MS word is available on your desktop for use.

Use MS Word Freely

If you don't want to buy Microsoft Office, you can download it for **free** from the Microsoft website. The online version of Word is brand new and does not have all of the functionality found in the desktop version. Because the website version cannot work when there is no internet connection, the offline/ desktop version is a viable option.

To use MS word freely online;

- visit their website, www.office.com.

- sign in if you have an existing account or

- create a new one if you do not have one, and MS word will be available for your use.

Opening And Pinning Ms Word

To open an MS word:

1. Type **Word** in your computer search bar.

2. Left-click on the word icon or **Open** to open a new MS word file.

3. You can also click any recent lists to open an already existing file.

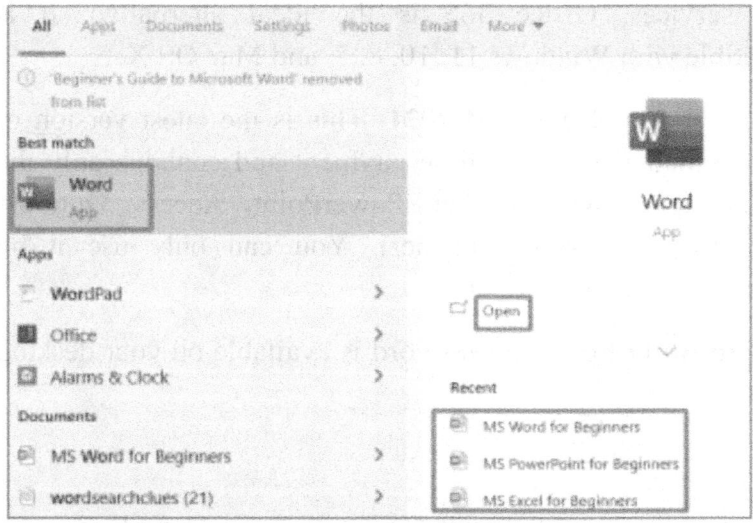

If you often use Word, it will be better to pin it to the start or taskbar.

To pin an MS Word to start or taskbar:

1. Right-click on the Word icon. A menu appears.

2. Select **Pin to Start** or **Pin to taskbar** as desired from the menu.

MS Word Start Screen

The start screen Home page appears when you first open MS Word, as illustrated below. A blue vertical bar on the left side of the page contains tabs to the right-side contents. The Home page has links to the shortcuts for the remaining tabs.

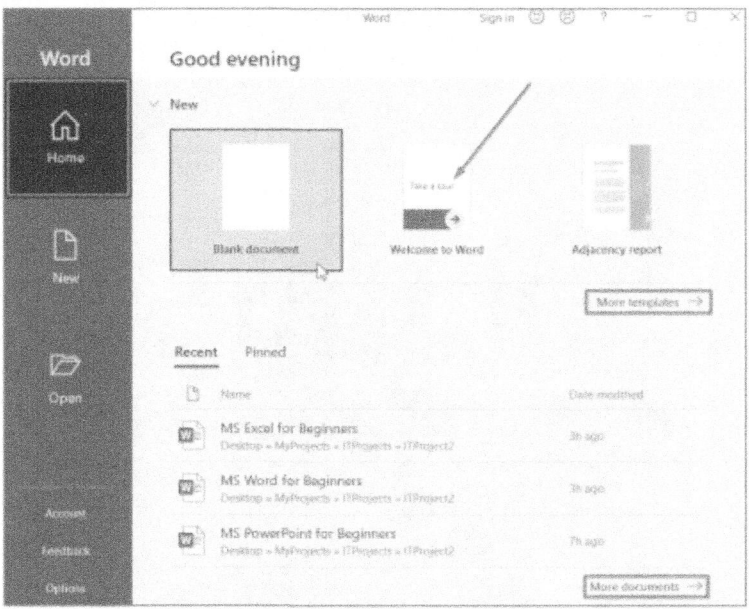

You have a **Blank** document on the **Home** screen that you can use to start from scratch. Also available are several learning tutorials and **templates** that can quickly get you started with MS Word. Click on more templates or the New tab at the left-hand bar if you want more templates.

Below the templates is the list of the **Recent** Word document. The **Open** tab at the left-sidebar or the **More documents** link opens more available documents at the right bottom corner of the list. Frequently open documents can be pinned and accessed in the **Pinned** beside the **Recent** list.

Chapter 2. Introduction To Microsoft Word

Microsoft Word is most likely used by practically everyone. This is due to the prevalence of word processing tasks in our daily life. A word processor may assist you in the creation of letters, memos, reports, and even emails, which are all commonplace in our everyday life. Word processors are capable of swiftly and easily editing, altering, and rearranging text.

As a result, you'll discover the fundamentals of Microsoft Word 2024 in this chapter, as well as how to use the most crucial features and capabilities that will help you compose documents quickly.

Note: Microsoft Word can be found in the Microsoft Office Suite and there are other applications in the Microsoft Suite Office, such as Microsoft Excel, Microsoft PowerPoint, Microsoft OneNote, Microsoft Outlook, Microsoft Access, and Microsoft Publisher. However, we're only going to focus on just Microsoft Word.

The Concept of Microsoft Word 2024

Microsoft Word is a word processing program developed by Microsoft in 1983 to assist individuals in writing. It works on a computer, desktop, laptop, or mobile device. It is a component of the Microsoft Office suite, which is utilized by a variety of people, including teachers, students, professionals, business owners, and people of various ages and backgrounds. It's used to create professional-looking documents, such as letters, reports, and resumes. Another benefit of a word processor is that it makes it simple to make modifications such as spelling corrections, additions, deletions, formatting, and text movement. Once the document is complete, it may be swiftly and correctly printed, as well as stored for future modifications.

Features of Microsoft Word 2024

Microsoft Word has different versions from its inception. But what makes the Microsoft word 2024 version unique include;

- **Simplified Word Processing** - Make, manage, and even edit documents without ever having to work hard. Users from all over the world use Microsoft Word to make and share all of their documents and this current version makes it easier to achieve this.

- **Rapid Document Editing** – Make changes to documents with unmatched ease and speed. Correct a document's spelling, test its readability, and change its grammar with tools that are meant to make the document better.

- It lets you save any original file in a lot of different formats. .doc,.pdf,.txt,.rts,.dot,.wps, and many more formats which can be used to make documents.

- You may easily create visually appealing and well-designed papers. Because of this fantastic user interface! Microsoft Word offers a user-friendly interface that allows even the most inexperienced computer users to create excellent documents.

Getting Microsoft Word 2024

It is possible to get Microsoft Word 2024 applications in various ways:

- The first option, which is common with students, is to buy a license and then download and install Word on your computer. This option is often selected by students because Microsoft gives a big discount to students.

- The second option is to pay for a year's worth of service (Office 365).

- Another alternative is to utilize Microsoft Word online. You can use the online version of Word for free, but you must access it through your browser. You will, however, require a Microsoft Word 365 account, and the online version will only allow you to access documents saved on your OneDrive.

Components Of Microsoft Word 2024

Now, let's talk about the components or parts of MS Word. These features let you do a lot of different things with your documents, like save, delete, style, modify, or look at the content of your documents.

1. **The File**: It has options like New, which is used to make a new document; Open (which is used to open an existing document); Save, which is used to save documents; Save As (which is used to rename a document and save it, info, options etc.

2. **The Home Tab**: The "Home" tab in MS Word is the first tab you see when you open the software. The Clipboard, Font, Style, and Editing are the most common groupings. It allows you to customize the color, font, emphasis, bullets, and location of your text. Aside from that, it has the ability to cut, copy, and paste. You will have additional alternatives to work with after hitting the home tab.

i. **Insert:** This part can be used to input anything into your document. Examples of things you can insert are tables, words, shapes, hyperlinks, charts, signature lines, time, shapes, headers, footers, text boxes, links, boxes, equations, and so on.

ii. **Draw:** Freehand drawing can be done with this tool in Ms. Word. Different types of pens for drawing are shown on this tab

iii. **Design**: Here, you can choose from documents with centred titles, off-centered headings, left-justified text and more. You can also select from different page borders, watermarks, and colors in the design tab.

iv. **Layout**: You can use it to make your Microsoft Word documents look the way you want them to look. It has options to set margins, show line numbers, set paragraph indentation, apply themes, control page orientation and size, line breaks, and more.

v. **The References Tab:** This option allows you to add references to a document and then create a bibliography at the end of the text for easy reference. The references are frequently maintained in a master list that may be used to add references to other documents. It has features such as a table of contents, footnotes, citations, and bibliography, as well as captions, an index, a table of authorities, and a smart look.

vi. **Review:** The Review Tab has commenting, language, translation, spell check, word count, and other tools for you to use. A good thing about it is that you can find and change comments very quickly. These options will display when you click on the review tab.

vii. **Mailing:** One of the best things about Microsoft Word is that you can write a letter, report, etc and send it to a lot of people at the same time, with each person's name and address in the letter.

viii. **View**: In the View tab, you can switch between a single page and a double page. You can also change how the layout tools work. You can use it to make a print layout, outline, website, task pane, toolbar, and rulers, as well as to make a full-screen view, zoom in and out, and so on.

Getting Into Microsoft Word

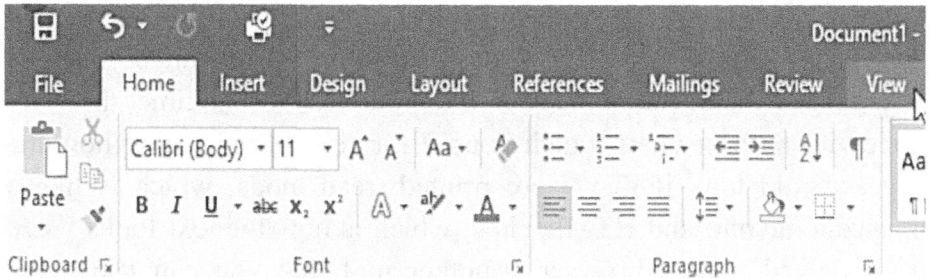

The Word Environment

The Quick Access Toolbar

The Quick Access Toolbar has icons for the tools you use the most. You can add buttons to this bar that you use a lot, and you can make them bigger.

The Ribbon

The Word Ribbon is an essential component of the Word interface. It can take the shape of an improper button, input box, or menu.

The Ribbon is separated into tabs, each of which has its own group of commanding buttons. The ribbon can be used in a variety of ways. You can find what you need by clicking on a tab and then looking through the group names. Finally, press the button to activate the command.

The Status Bar

This is a bar that shows up at the bottom of Word's window. It has information and icons on the left and right sides. The information on the left shows how many pages and how many words are in the text.

You can work with grammar and spelling tools by clicking the grammar icon.

Across the right side of the status bar, some icons can be used to change how the document is shown to you. Most of the time, there are three views: Print view, which is used for editing and seeing how the pages would look if they were printed; read mode, which is like a magazine layout; and HTML view, which is how the text looks when it is viewed with a browser. Another tool that you can use while viewing a document on the right side is a zoom slider. This lets you change the size of the document as you look at it.

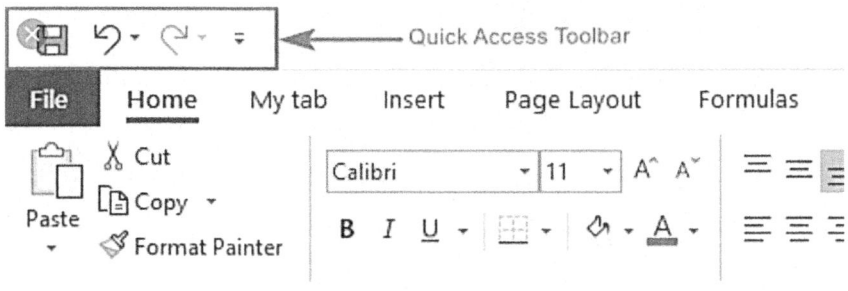

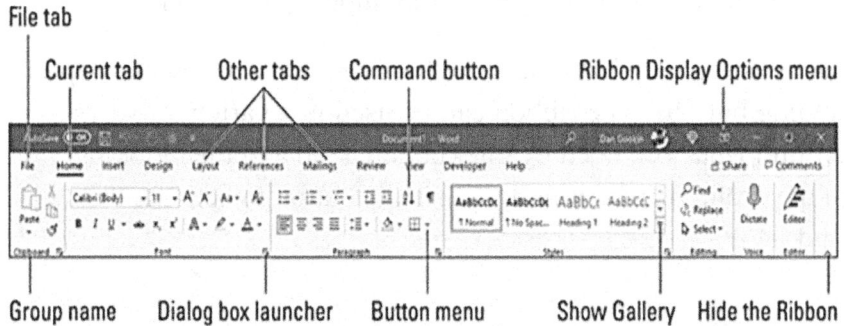

Starting The Word Program

First, you will need to find and open Microsoft Word (MS) on your computer.

From the computer's home screen:

- Double-click on the MS Word icon if it's on your computer's home screen.

But if it's not on your home screen, then do the following:

- Find the Start menu.

- Then click on Programs.

- Then click on Word, 2024.

Note: Keep in mind that Microsoft Word may be found in the Microsoft Office folder. If this is the case, the first thing you need do is click on Microsoft Office before clicking on "Word." Then you'll see a blank document where you may write your content and do various things with it.

Working On The Word Start Screen

Start screen: You can use it to open an already-opened document, start a new document from a template, or begin from scratch with a blank document. Choose to start a new document once and open it. Then, start writing.

Opening A New Document

- To open a document:

- Choose **File tab** on the ribbon and click on the **Open option**.

- Then the screen opens where you can click the blank document to start a new document

- The document is opened and shown on the screen. It's ready for anything.

Note: You can save the document and when you save a document for the first time, you give it a name.

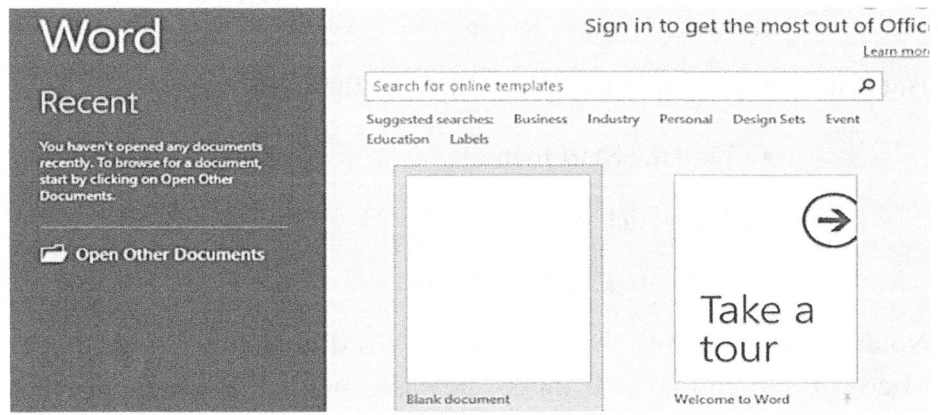

A View of a Document on Ms word

Changing The Size Of Text

A zoom command can help you enlarge or shrink a presentation, making it easier to see what you're looking at. You don't have to change the font size to make the information in Word bigger. To zoom in or out, go to the Zoom command as shown.

Employee Name	Customer Achieved (2018)	Sales (INR)
Vihan Aryan	200	100,000
Taijul Sharma	30	30,000
Advait Nagrwal	95	
Mohsin Pinjari	188	376,000

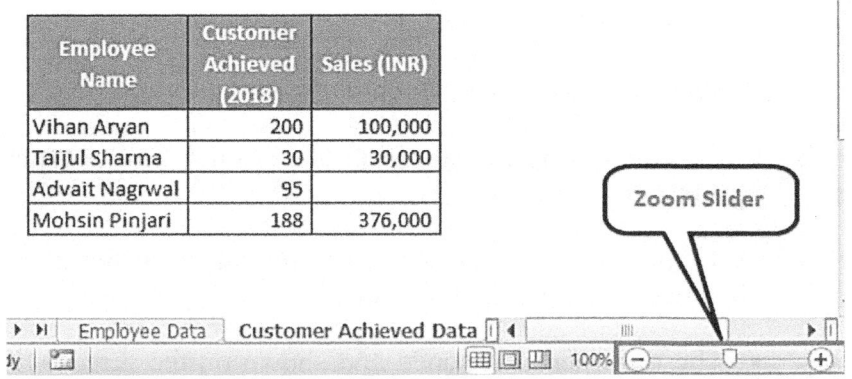

Quitting Word

When you're finished with a word processor and don't expect to use it again soon, it's best to close it. Select the "X" icon in the upper right corner of the screen to do so.

Remember that you must shut all open word document windows before declaring that you are finished with the document. It's also a good practice to save your work before closing the word processor.

Setting The Word Aside

You can minimize your word document to work on other things on your computer The minimize button is on the upper right corner of the screen.

To shrink the word window to a button on the taskbar, click the **Minimize** button and it will be possible for you to do other things with your computer. To bring the word document back to the screen fully, then you can click on the maximize button. How the Minimize and maximize icon looks is shown in the figure. The first is the minimize icon and the second is the maximize icon.

Chapter 3.   Typing Documents

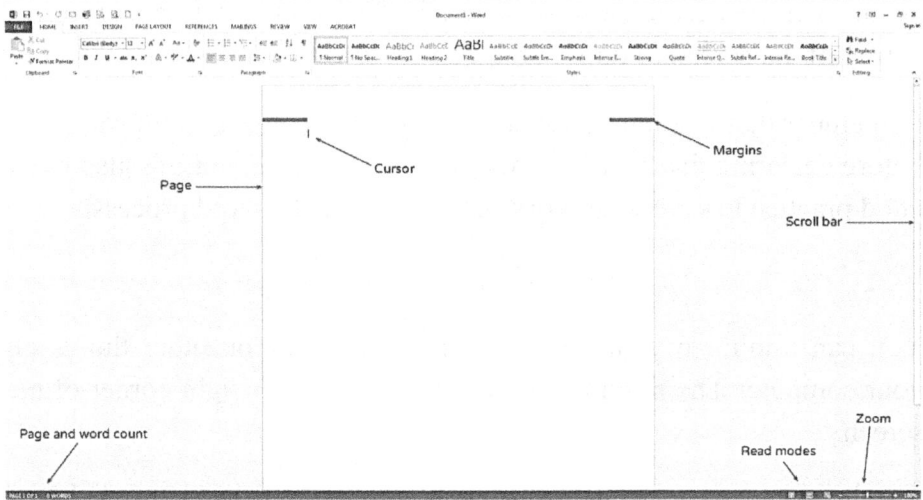

If there are no other gadgets that work with the computer, it will be useless. These diverse gadgets can be used to interface with the computer and do various tasks. This chapter will go over the two main typing input devices as well as everything about typing in Microsoft Word. The image above depicts how the typing screen appears.

Input Devices Set Up

You can enter information into a computer with a device called an input device. The two most important input device is the Keyboard and the Mouse. These two input devices are very important for you to be able to communicate with your computer.

1. The PC Keyboard

A computer keyboard is a piece of hardware that lets you type in data (text, number, punctuations, etc) and commands to a computer. In most cases, your keyboard is the best way to get information into your computer. You can type a letter, number, symbols, punctuation Mark's, etc and you do this by pressing the keys on your keyboard.

How the keys are put together

The keys on your keyboard can be broken down into different groups based on how they work:

- **Using (alphanumeric) keys to type.** These keys have the same letter, number, punctuation, and symbol keys that you would find on a typewriter.

- **The function keys.** The function keys are used to do certain things. They're called F1, F2, F3, and so on, until F12. These keys can do different things in different programs.

- **The navigation keys**. These keys are used to move around and alter text in documents and web pages. There is an arrow next to each of these buttons. The Home and End keys are also present.

- **The numeric keypad**. It makes it easy and fast to enter numbers. All the keys are in a block like on an old calculator or adding machine.

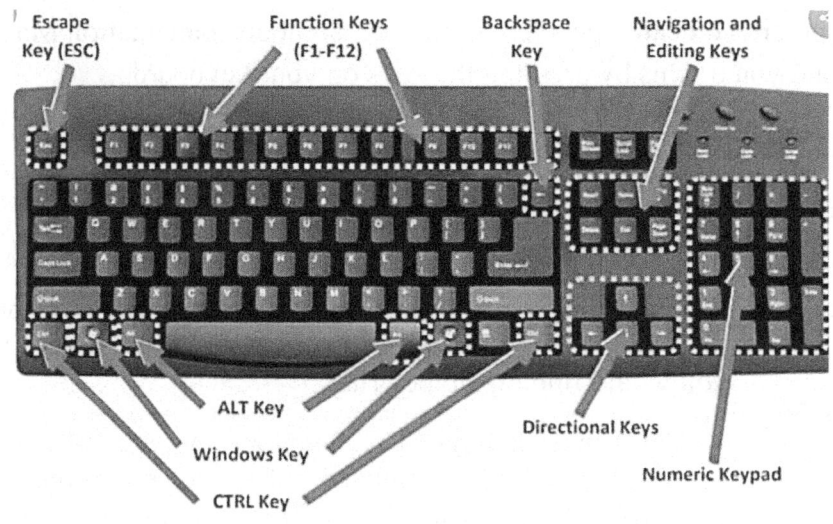

Some major keys in the keyboard are the Shift key, Caps lock, Tab, Enter key, Spacebar, Backspace, Alt key, Arrow Keys.

Note:

- There is a Desktop Keyboard and the Laptop Keyboard.

- Most laptop keyboards don't have a numeric keypad.

- The cursor keys are close together around the typewriter keys in weird and creative ways.

- The function keys may be accessed by pressing certain keys together.

- Each key has two symbols on it, which show that the person has two different personalities.

Putting Words on a Document

When you need to input something in a software, email, or text box, a vertical line blinks. The cursor or insertion point is this line. It indicates where the text you'll write will begin. You can move the cursor by using the mouse to click where you want it to go, or by using the keys. The four arrow keys that go up, down, left, and right can be used to move your cursor in Microsoft Word.

Using the Onscreen Keyboard

When you want to use the On-Screen Keyboard;

- Go to **Start** on your computer

- Then select **Settings**

- Click on **Ease of Access**

- And then click on the Keyboard and turn on the toggle next to Use the On-Screen Keyboard to use the keyboard on the screen

- Immediately, you will see a keyboard that you can use to move around the screen and type text. The keyboard will stay on the screen until you shut it down.

- Open a document in any program where you can write text. Then, with your mouse, click the keys on the onscreen keyboard to type in the text you want.

- To close it, Choose "Close" and then click "OK" on the screen keyboard to get rid of it from your screen.

Note: Here are some things to note about using an on-screen keyboard:

- The onscreen keyboard is nearly identical to a physical keyboard. You can type with your fingers, but you won't be able to do so as rapidly as you would on a real keyboard.

- Some of the special keys (function keys, cursor keys, and so on) are hard to get to. Some of the time, you can get them by switching to a different touchscreen keyboard layout, but most of the time, they're not there at all.

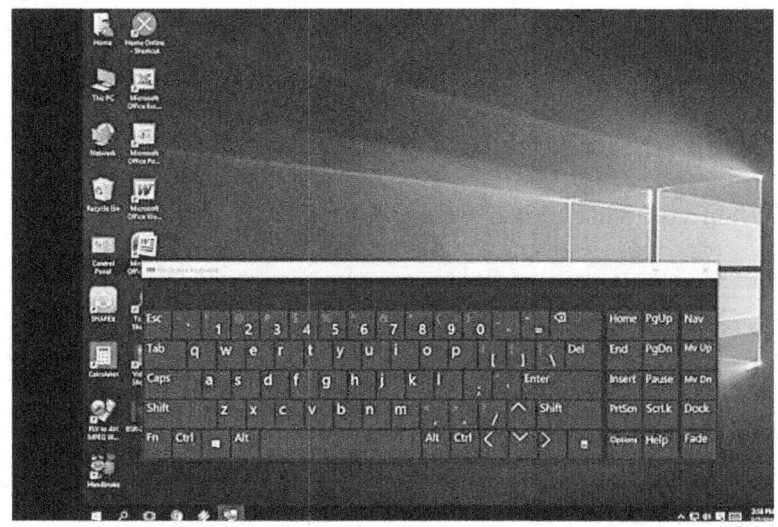

- Using the Ctrl key on the onscreen keyboard requires two steps: first, tap the Ctrl key, and then tap another key.

- Some of the Ctrl-key combinations in Word can't be made by using the on-screen keyboard.

2. The Mouse

The mouse is yet another input device that can be used to type or enter commands into Microsoft Word. You can move the cursor or pointer on a computer screen by dragging it across a flat surface, such as your desk or table, with a mouse. The name "mouse" came to be known as "mouse" because it resembles a little, corded, oval-shaped instrument. Some mice contain built-in functions, such as extra buttons that may be programmed and utilized for various purposes.

Early mouse devices were connected to computers by a cable or cord and had a roller ball built-in as a movement sensor on the bottom of the device. While modern mouse devices are now optical technology, this signifies that a visible or invisible light beam is used to move the cursor. Many models have wireless connectivity through radio frequency (RF) and Bluetooth, among other technologies.

26

The three main types of the mouse are:

- **Mechanical:** The mouse has a trackball under it and mechanical sensors that make it easy to move in all directions.

- **Optomechanical**: The same as mechanical, but optical sensors instead of mechanical ones are used to detect the movement of the trackball.

- **Optical:** The most expensive. It has no moving parts, uses a laser to detect movement, and reacts faster than previous varieties.

Understanding How The Mouse Pointer Works

A mouse pointer, also called a cursor, is a visible item that shows up on a computer screen. Computer users can move the mouse pointer around the screen by moving the mouse, which moves the mouse pointer. You can move around the document and select text with it too.

The mouse pointer on a computer is typically in the shape of an arrow or a hand. The arrow usually points to the top of the screen and tilts slightly to the left. Arrows represent where the mouse is on the screen, and a line-like pointer shows where text can be inserted in graphical user interfaces. Instead of arrows or hands, text-based interfaces can utilize a rectangle to show where items are.

Cursors often change how they look on a screen because of how they are being used and manipulated on the screen.

- If you want to edit any text, the mouse pointer turns into an I-beam.

- In some documents, users might see hand cursors.

- Mouse pointer 11 o'clock is used to choose items.

- When you want to select lines of text, you use the mouse pointer at 1 o'clock to do it.

- In some document types, users might be able to press a mouse button and see that the pointer responds by "grabbing" the document page or an object in it.

- When the user is working with graphical editing software, the cursor might change to match the function that he or she is using.

Note: The mouse pointer changes when the click-and-type capability is enabled. Below the I-beam mouse pointer, tiny lines appear to the left and right of the mouse cursor. When you point your mouse at a word tool, you'll see a pop-up information bubble appear. The text in the bubble may provide some insight on how to utilize the command.

Also, in addition, As a person moves the mouse, the mouse pointer will move around the screen in the same way. When the mouse pointer is over a place where text can be typed, the pointer can blink as it thinks about typing. If a user wants to stop the cursor from blinking, he might be able to change the pointer's settings, such as how visible it is and how quickly it blinks. This will depend on the interface.

Keyboard "Do's and Don'ts."

Knowing how to type on a keyboard is essential since it will allow you to learn a few aspects about typing that are specific to word processing. Although learning to type is not required, it is recommended that you do so to avoid unnecessary stress.

i. Following the Insertion Pointer

The text you write in Word shows up where the insertion pointer is. As soon as you move the pointer, it looks like a moving vertical bar: When you move the insertion pointer, a character comes up in front of it one by one. It moves to the right after a character is added, making room for more text.

Note: The Insertion Point can be moved to a new place and the key moves the insertion point to wherever you want it to be.

ii. Pressing the Space Bar

The space bar is used to type blank lines in your text. The space bar is a key on a keyboard that looks like a long horizontal bar. It's in the bottom row, and it's significantly bigger than the rest of the keyboard's keys. You can use it to swiftly enter a space between words while typing.

When typing, the most important thing to remember about the space bar is that you only need to press it once. There is only one space in between words and after punctuation. That's everything!

Note: Any time you think you need two or more spaces in a document, use a tab instead. Tabs are the best way to indent text and to line up text in columns, so they are good for both.

iii. BackSpace and Delete Key

When you make a mistake while typing, you push the backspace key on your keyboard. It deletes a character by moving the insertion pointer back one character. The Delete key also deletes text, but only to the right of the insertion pointer, so it doesn't completely erase it.

iv. Pressing The Enter Key

The Return key is another name for it. It's the keyboard key that tells the computer to enter the line of data or instruction that was just typed into the computer. You only use the Enter key in word processing when you've reached the end of a sentence.

Note: If your text reaches too near to the right margin in Word, it will automatically transfer your last words to the following line. You don't have to press Enter at the end of a line because of this word-wrap feature.

During The Time You Type, Things Happen.

As you type your text quickly, with your fingers pounding the keys on the keyboard, you might see a few things on the screen. You may see spots. lines and boxes that may appear. We are going to look at some major stuff that happens when you type

i. Text Prediction

Microsoft Word helps you write faster as you type. As you type, the app anticipates your next words and presents them for you to accept, allowing you to go through your manuscript faster than ever before. Continue typing after accepting the suggested text with the Tab or Right-arrow key on your keyboard. Simply continue typing or press Esc to dismiss the recommendation.

ii. Keep an Eye on the Status Bar.

A status bar is a type of graphical control element that shows a section of information at the bottom of a window. As you type, it shows you how your document is doing. The status bar shows a collection of information that starts at the left end and moves right.

The information that shows up on the status bar can be changed. It talks about how to control what shows up on the status bar and how to hide things.

It can be broken up into sections so that you can group information. Its main job is to show information about the current state of its window, but some status bars have extra features. For example, many web browsers have sections that can be clicked on to show security or privacy information.

Some good things about status bars: They let you see messages and the whole screen at the same time, they let you write while you look at your status data, status data is shown in a way that lets you see other menu options at the same time and they show how things are going at all times.

iii. Notice the Page Breaks.

A page break in your text indicates where the current page ends and the following one begins. After that, you can click anywhere to open a new page. Click the Insert tab at the top of the screen to add a page break. The Page Break button is on the right of the screen in the Pages group; click it to make the page break visible.

Inserting Page Breaks Manually

It's best to put your insertion point where you want the page break to be. To change the layout of your page, click on the Page Layout ribbon. Then click on Breaks and then choose Page. Page break becomes visible.

Note: The Pages group has a button called "Blank Page." If you want to add a blank page at the break, click on that button.

Remove the Page Break

A page break you put in now can be taken out at any time if you change your mind.

To find and remove page breaks quickly, you should first show the formatting marks.

- Click the **Home button.**

- The **Show/Hide button i**s on the right.

- This shows punctuation characters like spaces, paragraph markers, and the most important for this lesson, page and section breaks.

- Double-click the **page brea**k to pick it up.

- Press the **delete key.**

- The page break is gone.

iv. Collapsible Headers

While typing, you may notice a little triangle to the left of some of your document's headings. You can modify the size of all the text in the header section with these triangles. To hide the text, click once; to reveal it, click twice.

The page does not appear to be empty because of the collapsed sections. They do an excellent job at reducing the size of the page to make it easier to read.

vi. Getting Rid of Spots and Clutter in the Text

Seeing dots or spots in your writing does not necessarily indicate that something is wrong. Characters that can't be read are what you're seeing. Spaces, tabs, the Enter key, and other symbols are used in Word to represent items that are normally hidden. When the Show/Hide feature is enabled, these dots and tittles appear. If you need to remove them again, simply click the Show/Hide button.

vi. Understanding the Colors of the Underlines

When Word underlines your text without your permission, it's alerting you to something that's not right with the way things are going. These underlines are not text styles. At times, you might see these:

- **Red zigzag**: This indicate there is a mistake in the word

- **Blue zigzag**: It indicates errors in grammar and word choice

- **Blue single line**: When you write a document, Word adds blue underlined text to show where web page addresses are. You can press Ctrl+click the blue text to go to the web page.

- **Red lines:** You might see red lines in the margin, below text, or even through text. It means that you're using Track Changes in Word.

Chapter 4.   Editing on Microsoft Word 2024

Making text is what typing is all about. Going through and revising your words is also a part of the process. Word contains many commands that can cut, slice, stitch, and so on to assist you with text editing. The instructions are a crucial aspect of word processing, and they perform best when dealing with large amounts of text. Writing initially and then editing is a smart strategy.

Therefore, this chapter will cover how to edit text, how to delete lines and sentences, splitting and joining paragraphs, how to use the Redo command to undo what you did, etc will all be discussed in this chapter.

Deleting a Single Character

When you write in Word, you can use the keyboard to both add and remove text. There are a lot of keys that make text but Backspace and Delete are the only keys that can delete text. These keys become more powerful when they are used with other keys, or even the mouse, that help them delete large amounts of text.

- **The Delete key** removes characters to the **righ**t of the insertion pointer

- **The backspace key** deletes characters to the **left** of the insertion pointer.

Deleting a Word

The Ctrl and Backspace or Delete keys can be used to delete an entire planet. These keyboard shortcuts can be used in two ways. When the insertion pointer is at the beginning or end of a word, they operate best. When the pointer is in the middle of a word, delete commands are utilized. These commands only delete from that middle point to the start or end of the word. The shortcut to delete is illustrated as;

- The word to the leftward of the insertion pointer is deleted when you press **Ctrl+Backspace.**

- The word to the rightward of the insertion pointer is deleted when you press **Ctrl + Delete.**

Note: When you use Ctrl+Backspace to delete a word to the left. The pointer is at the end of what comes before it. When you use Ctrl+Delete to remove a word, the cursor moves to the start of the next word. This is done to make it easier to quickly remove several words in a row.

Deleting More Than a Word

The keyboard and mouse must work together to remove chunks of text that are bigger than a single letter or single word. The first step is to choose a chunk of text and then delete that chunk of text.

Remove a Line of Text

A line of text starts on one side of the page and goes to the other. If you want to remove the line, you can:

- Make sure the mouse pointer is next to a line of text by moving it to the left.

- Then click on the mouse.

- The line of text is chosen and is shown in a different color on the screen.

- Press the delete key to eliminate that line.

Delete a Sentence

A sentence is a group of text that begins with a capital letter and ends with a period, question mark, or exclamation point, depending on what you're trying to communicate. To do this;

- Place the mouse pointer where the sentence you want to delete lies.

- Press then hold down the Ctrl key at the same time as you click the mouse.

- Using Ctrl and a mouse click together, you can choose a sentence of text that you want to delete.

- The Ctrl key can be let go of, and then you can hit delete.

Deleting a Paragraph

A Paragraph is a group of sentences formed when you press the Enter key. If you want to delete a whole paragraph quickly, here's how to do it:

- Click the mouse **three times.** In this case, the triple-click selects the whole paragraph of the text.

- Press the **Delete button.**

Another way to select a paragraph is to click the mouse two times in the left margin, next to the paragraph, to make it select and then click on delete.

Deleting a Page

Page of text is everything on a page from top to bottom. This part of the document isn't one that Word directly addresses with keyboard commands. To get rid of a whole page of text, you'll need some sleight of hand. Take these steps:

- Press the keys **Ctrl+G.**

- The Find and Replace dialogue box comes up, with the Go To tab at the top of the list of tabs.

- On the Go to What list, choose Page and then type the number of the page you want to remove.

- Click the Go To button, then the Close button. And the page shows up.

- Press the **Delete** button.

- All of the text on the page is taken off.

Split and Join Paragraphs

A paragraph as earlier defined is a group of sentences that all say the same thing about a thought, idea, or theme. In Word, a paragraph is a chunk of text that ends when you press the Enter key. In a document, you can change a paragraph by splitting or joining text.

To split a single paragraph in two;

When you need to start a new paragraph, move the cursor to the desired location. That point belongs at the start of a sentence. To begin, press the Enter key. Word splits the text in half during this process. The paragraph above the insertion pointer becomes the current paragraph, while the paragraph below it becomes the next paragraph.

Making A Single Paragraph Out Of Two Separate Ones

To join two paragraphs together and make them one, simply do this; When you place the insertion pointer at the start of the second paragraph or use the keyboard or click the mouse to move the insertion pointer where you want it to be then press the Backspace button.

This implies that you have removed the entered character from the paragraph before this one thus making two paragraphs into one.

Soft and Hard Return

The **Return or Enter key** is pressed at the end of each line when typing on a keyboard. This indicates that you've finished one paragraph and are ready to go on to the next. However. When you set your page margins, Word knows that when you get to the right margin, your text should wrap to the next line automatically.

There may be times, though, when you wish to stop writing a line before it reaches the right margin. In these situations, you have two options for terminating a line. The first way is to type in the end point of the line and then press Enter. As a result, the document has a hard return on it. This action (pressing Enter) indicates that you've reached the end of a paragraph and want to start a new one.

Another approach to end a line is to hit **Shift+Enter,** which will insert a soft return, also known as a line break or newline character, into the document. The end of a paragraph is indicated by hard returns, whereas the end of a line is indicated by **soft returns.**

A hard return displays on your screen as a paragraph mark (a backward P), while a soft return appears as a down-and-left pointing arrow.

The Undo Command

The Undo command can undo anything you do in Word, like changing text, moving blocks, typing, and deleting text. It does this for everything you do in the program. If you want to use the Undo command, you have two ways to do it:

- The shortcut method is to Press **Ctrl+Z.**

- Alternatively, you can click the Undo command button on the Quick Access toolbar to get back to where your previous work is.

Note: In some cases, you can't use the Undo command because there's nothing to undo. For example, you can't go back and undo a file save.

The Redo Command

If you make a mistake and accidentally undo something, use the Redo command to restore things to their previous state. Assume you type some text and then use Undo to erase it. And, you can use the Redo command to go back and type again. It's your choice. You can choose

- The shortcut method is to press **Ctrl+Y.**

- Alternatively, take a look at the **Quick Access toolbar** and click the **Redo button.**

Note: The Undo command does the opposite of what the Redo command does. So, if you write text, Undo removes the text, and Redo puts the text back.

The Repeat Command

To repeat what you did in Word last time, use the Repeat command to do the same thing again. This could be typing new text, formatting it, or doing a lot of other things.

Using the Repeat command, you can keep the same picture. Whenever there is no more to redo, the Redo command turns into the Repeat command.

To do this:

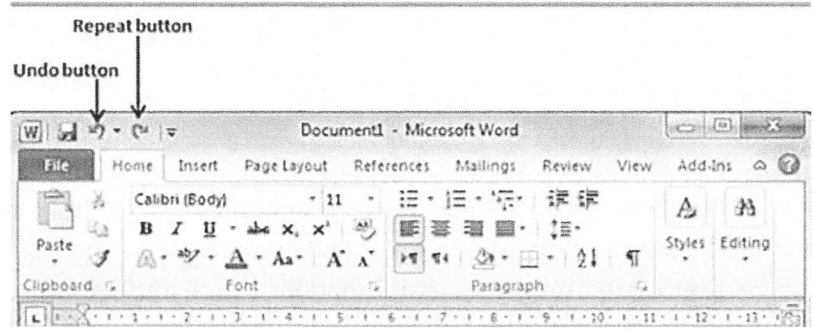

- The shortcut method is to Press **Ctrl+Y**, which is the same keyboard shortcut as to redo something.

Finally, now that you know how to utilize Word's fundamental tools to create a document, this chapter has covered several additional editing tools and easy formatting effects to improve the appearance of a document. Other chapters will go through other editing tools.

Chapter 5.   Document Formatting

Formatting With Styles And Themes

Styles and **themes** are powerful Word features that you can quickly and easily use to create a professional-looking document. A **style** is a Word predefined combination of all font, and paragraph formatting elements (e.g., font size, font type, color, indent, etc.) applied to a selected text or paragraph. At the same time, a **theme** is a group of formatting choices with a unique set of colors, font, and effects to change the appearance of the entire document.

You can choose from a variety of styles and themes in Word. The steps for applying, modifying, and creating styles and themes are outlined here.

Applying, Modifying, And Creating Styles

To apply a style:

> 1. Select the text or paragraph you want to apply a style.
>
> 2. Go to the **Home** ribbon.
>
> 3. Select the style you want in the **Style** group. You can hover over each style to see the live effect in your document before applying. To see the additional style, click the **More** dropdown arrow.

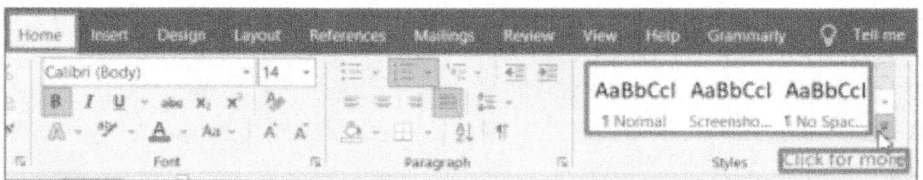

To modify a style:

> 1. Select the style you want to modify.
>
> 2. Right-click and select Modify in the dropdown list.

A **Modify Style** dialog box appears.

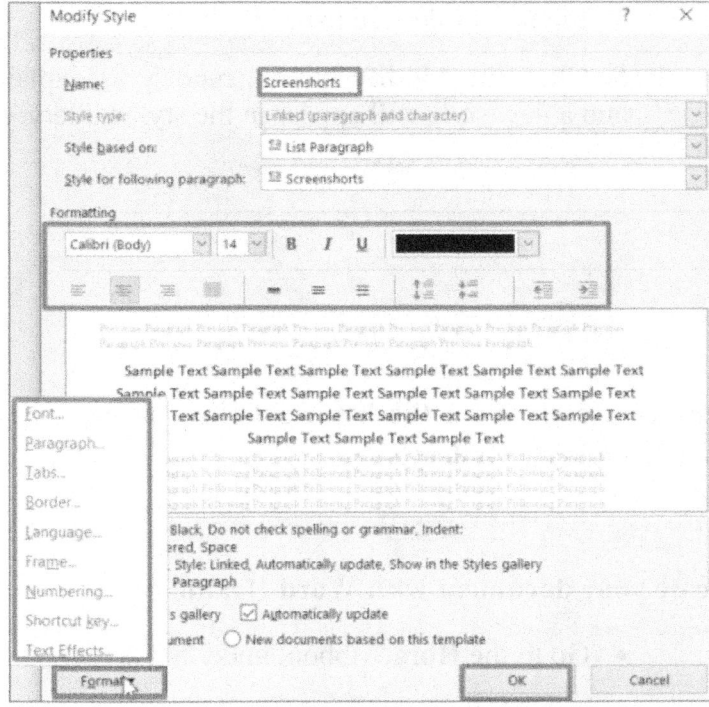

3. Set as desired all the formatting groups. You can as well change the style name.

4. Click on the **Format** button for more formatting options and control.

5. Check the **Automatically update** box to update the styles changes anywhere you have applied them in your document.

6. Press **OK** when you are done.

To create a style:

1. Go to the **Home** ribbon.

2. In the **Style** group, click the **More** dropdown arrow.

3. Select **Create a Style**.

A dialog box appears.

4. Input your desired name.

5. Click the **Modify** button, modify as explained above, and a new style will appear in the style gallery.

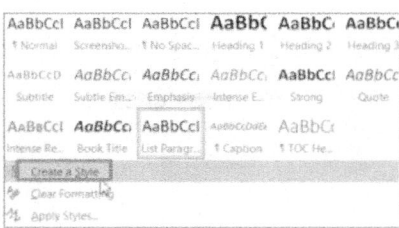

To remove a style from the list, right-click on the style and select **Remove from Style Gallery.**

Creating Your Document With Word Headings

To create your document with Word Headings:

- Go to the **Home** ribbon, under **Style** group.

- Select all your chapters or section headings and click **Heading 1** in the **Style** group.

- Select all the sub-topics or sub-sections and click **Heading 2** in the **Style** group.

- Select all your sub-sub-topics and click **Heading 3** in the **Style** group. Continue to your last headings.

You can customize your headings following the steps in **Section 7.1.1**

Changing, Customizing, And Saving A Theme

A theme is a collection of colors, fonts, and effects that alter the overall appearance of your page. The default Office theme is used whenever you create a document in Word.

To change the theme of your document:

1. Click the **Design** tab.

2. Click the **Themes** command in the **Document Formatting** group.

A drop-down list appears.

3. Hover your cursor over a theme to preview it in your document.

4. Click your desired theme to apply it.

Customizing a theme

You can change any theme element (i.e., color, font, and effect) to create a unique look for your document.

To change themes colors:

1. Go to the **Design** tap.

2. Select **Colors** command.

A drop-down color palette appears.

3. Select the desired color palate or click customize color to combine your colors.

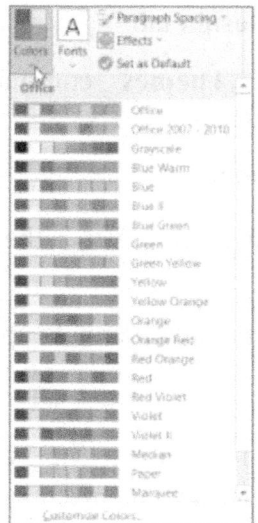

To change a theme font:

1. Go to the **Design** tab.

2. Click the **Font** command.

A drop-down menu of fonts appears.

3. Select your desired theme fonts or

Select **Customize Font** to customize your font. Set your desired font in the dialog box that appears and press **Ok**.

To change a theme effect:

1. Go to the **Design** tab.

2. Click the **Effect** command.

A drop-down list of all the available effects appears.

3. Select the desired effect. You can see the live preview of any effect you hover on.

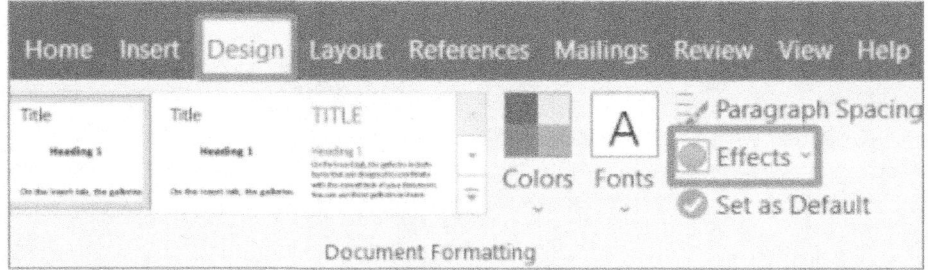

You can save your current or customized theme for later use.

To save a theme:

1. Click the **Design** tab.

2. Click the **Themes** command in the **Document Formatting** group.

A drop-down list appears.

3. Select **Save Current Theme**.

4. Input a file name for your theme and press **Save** in the dialog box that appears.

Setting Paper Size, Margins, And Orientation

Margins are the spaces between the edges of your document (top, bottom, left, and right) and your text. They make your work look professional. The default margin in Word is 1 inch for all sides. There are predefined margins, and you can as well customize your margins.

To apply a predefined margin to your document:

1. Go to the **Layout** ribbon.

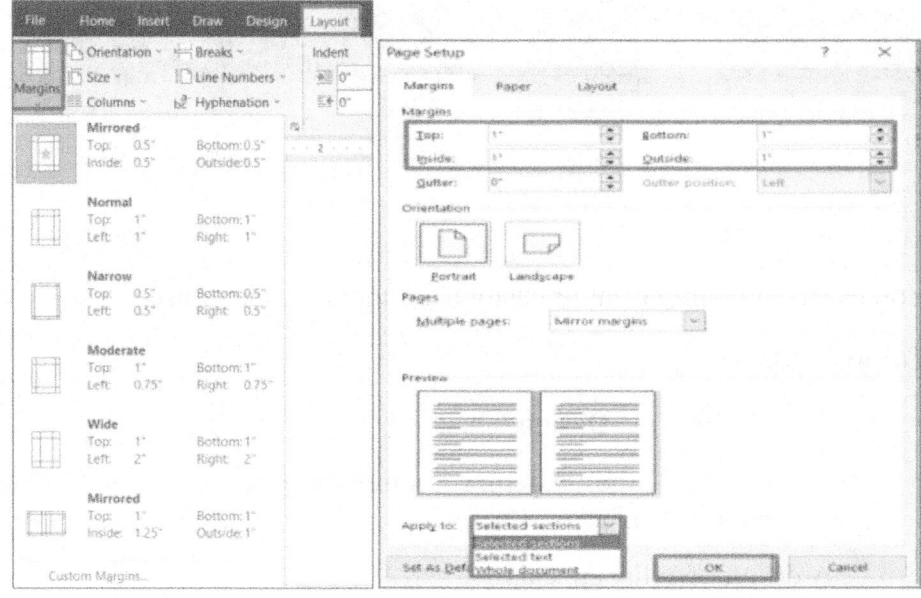

2. Choose **Margins** in the **Page Setup** group.

A drop-down menu appears.

3. Select an option from the list.

To customize your margin:

3. Select **Custom Margins...**

A dialog box appears.

4. Input your values in the textboxes,

5. Select an option in **Apply to:** box.

6. Click **Set As Default** (optional)

7. Press **OK.**

Note: Select the whole document first before applying a predefined margin to a document with different sections because Word applies the predefined margin only to the current section.

PAGE SIZE

To set Page Size:

1. Go to the **Layout** ribbon.

2. Click the **Size** button.

A drop-down menu appears.

3. Select an option from the list.

To customize your page size:

3. Select **More Paper Sizes...**

A dialog box appears.

4. Input your values in the Width and Height text boxes.

5. Select an option in **Apply to:** box.

6. Click **Set As Default** if you wish to set the size as default.

7. Press **OK.**

PAGE ORIENTATION:

To change your page orientation:

1. Go to the **Layout** ribbon.

2. Click the **Orientation** command.

A drop-down menu appears.

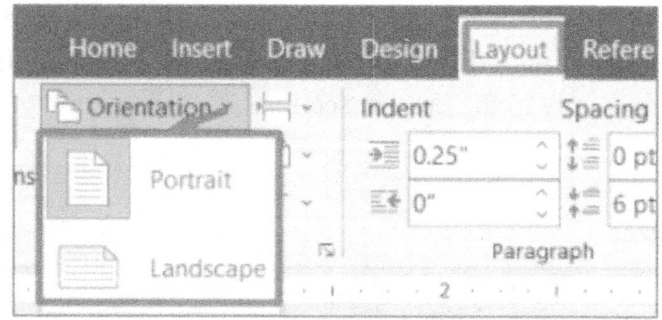

3. Select **Portrait** for a vertical page or **Landscape** for a horizontal page.

Page Breaks And Section Breaks

When working on a document with multiple pages and numerous headings, it might be difficult to format the text so that all chapter heads begin on a new page rather than at the bottom of the previous page. It may also be difficult to add separate headers, footers, footnotes, page numbers, and other formatting elements to some types of documents having several sections, such as an article, report, paper, or book.

Word repeats the headers, footers, and footnotes, as well as the numbering, across the document. Document breaks are required to have a separate one.

There are two types of documents breaks in Word:

- Page breaks

- Section breaks.

Page breaks partition the document's body while section breaks partition not only the document body but also the headings (or chapters), headers, footers, footnotes, page numbers, margins, etc.

Page Breaks are subdivided into:

- **Page break**: This forces all the text behind the insertion point to the next page.

- **Column** break: This forces the text to the right of the insertion point to the next column of the same page when working with a document with multiple columns

- **Text Wrapping break**: It moves any text to the right of the cursor to the following line, and it is instrumental when working with objects.

Section Breaks are subdivided into:

- **Next Page break:** This separates the papers by adding another page with its own formatting. This is helpful for dividing your document into chapters with various headers, footers, page numbers, and so on.

- **Continuous break:** This divides the document into sections that can be independently formatted on the same page without creating a new page. This type of break is usually used to change the number of columns on a page.

- **Even Page break:** This shifts the insertion point and any text at its right to the next even page.

- **Odd Page break**: This shifts the insertion point and any text at its right to the next odd page.

To Insert a Page Break or Section Break:

1. Place your insertion point to where you want the break.

2. Go to the **Layout** ribbon.

3. Select **Breaks** in the **Page Setup** group.

A drop-down list appears with all the types of breaks.

4. Select from the options the type of section break you want.

Inserting Header Or Footer

A header is a piece of text that appears at the top of each page of a document. A footer, on the other hand, is a text that is put to the bottom margin to provide information about the document, such as the title, page number, image, logo, and so on.

To place a Header or Footer to your document:

1. Go to the **Insert** ribbon.

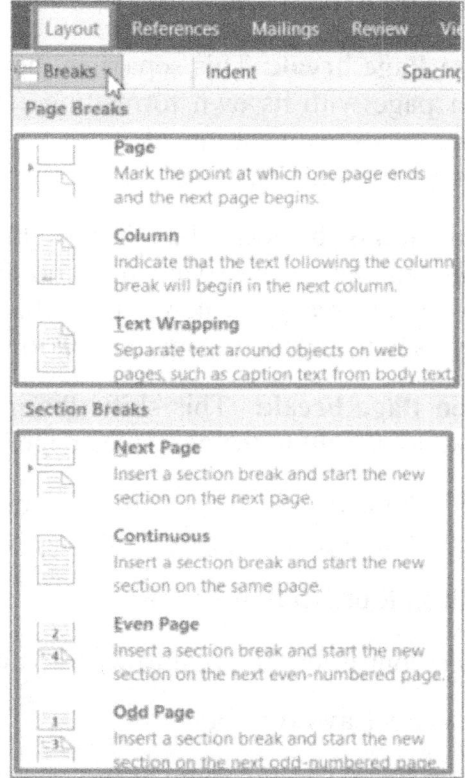

2. Select **Header** or **Footer** command.

A drop-down menu appears with header or footer styles.

3. Click on the desired style.

Word activates the top and bottom margin for your header or footer insertion.

4. Replace the text with your desired text.

5. Click on the **Close Header and Footer** command when you are done.

Alternatively,

1. Double-click in the top or bottom margin to activate the header and footer area.

2. Insert your footer or header.

3. Double click outside the margin area or press the **Esc** key to go back to your document.

You can always use the above method to edit your header or footer. Also available is a contextual **Design** tab you can use to design your header or footer.

To delete your header or footer, just delete the text and close the header and footer.

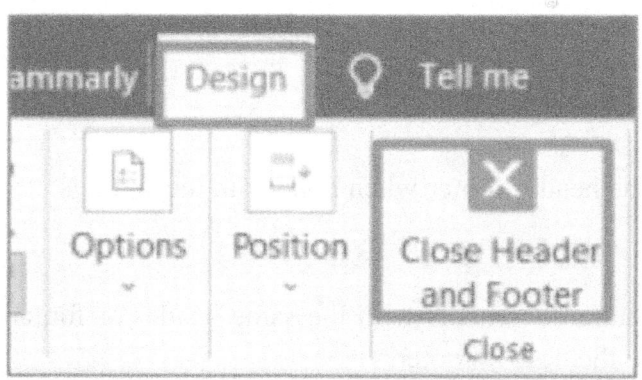

Inserting Different Headers or Footers in Word

To insert a separate Header or Footer for a Separate Section:

1. Insert **Next Page** section breaks to where you want different headers or footers to start.

2. Activate the headers or footers of each section.

In the **Navigation** group of the **Header & Footer** Tools ribbon;

3. Deselect the **Link to Previous** button to disconnect the sections.

4. Add the header or footer for each section or chapter.

5. To put a different header on the first page of the document or a section, Check the **Different First Page** box.

6. To put a right-justified header for some pages and a left-justified header for some pages, check the **Different Odd & Even Pages** box.

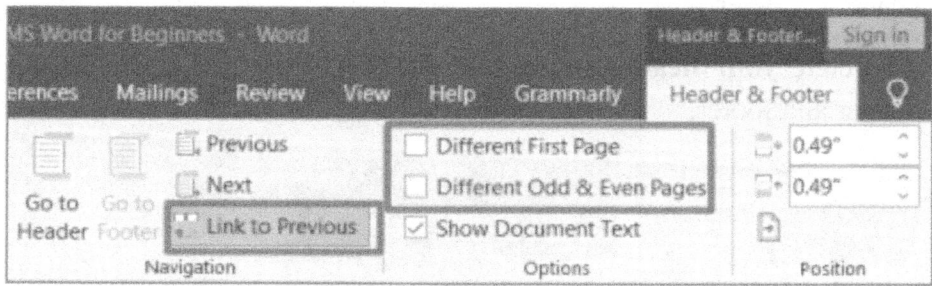

7. Close the header/footer when done with the settings.

Saving Headers Or Footers For Later Use

If you frequently generate documents with the same header or footer, it's a good idea to store the header/footer.

To save your header or footer for later use:

1. Activate and select all the header or footer contents you want to save.

2. Click the **Header** or **Footer** drop-down button as the case may be.

3. Select **Save Selection to Header Gallery** or **Save Selection to Footer Gallery,** depending on whether you select Header or Footer.

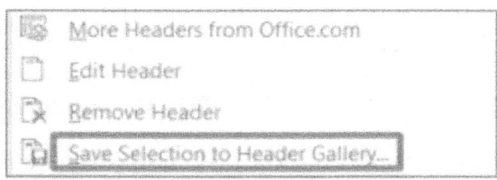

A dialog box appears.

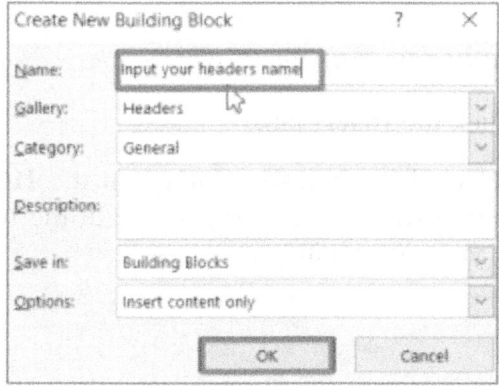

4. Input the name you want to give the header or footer and do any other desired settings.

5. Press **OK,** and your header or footer will be saved.

You can access and apply the header or footer at any time in the drop-down list of the **Header** or **Footer** drop button. You might have to scroll down to see your

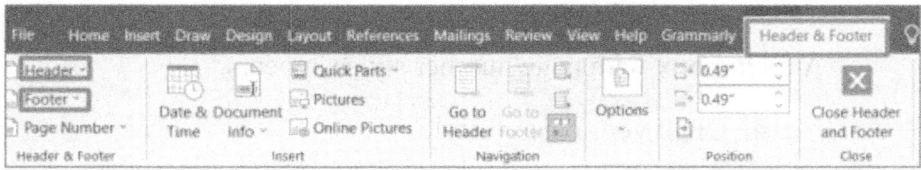

To delete your saved header or footer:

1. right-click on it.

2. Select Organize and Delete.

A dialog box appears highlighting the header or footer.

3. Click the **Delete** button.

4. Press **yes** to confirm the prompt that appears.

5. Press **Close** in the dialog box, and your header or footer will no longer be in the gallery.

Page Numbering

To add page number to your document:

1. Click the **Insert** tab.

2. Select **Page Number** button in the **Header & Footer** section. A drop-down menu appears with the list of where you can insert your page number.

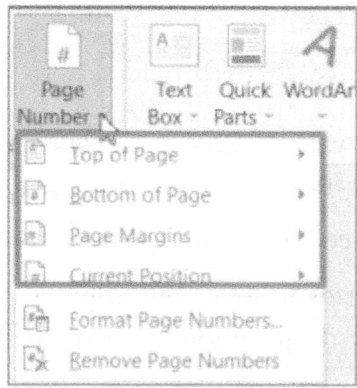

3. Select an option.

A dialog box with page number styles appears.

4. Click your desired style.

Word assigns page numbers to all of your document's pages and activates the header and footer areas.

5. Right-click on the page number or Click the **Page Number** command in the **Headers & Footers** ribbon for settings

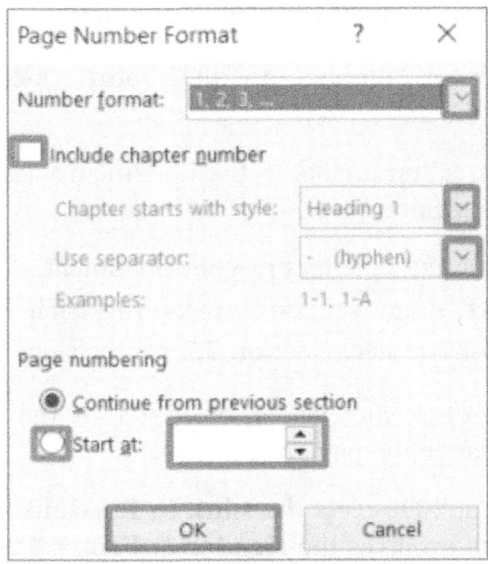

A dialog box appears.

6. Select the drop-down button to select the **Number format** you want.

7. Check the **Include chapter number** box to include chapter numbers, select the **Chapter starts with style** and **Use separator** options (optional).

8. Check the **Start at** button and set the start value if you do not want the numbering to continue from the previous section (applicable for setting different page numbering for different sections).

9. Press **OK**.

10.   Double click outside the margin to go back to your document area.

Inserting Different Page Numbers.

To insert different page numbers to your document:

1. Insert page number to the entire document first, following the above steps.

2. Create section breaks to the document where you want different page numbers.

If you have different chapters in your document, it is advisable to create **Next Page** section breaks for each chapter and prefatory sections. (Check **section 7.3** for the steps)

3. Double-click the header or footer of the section you want to change the page number.

4. Locate and Deselect the **Link to Previous** button in the **Navigation** group of the **Header & Footer Tools** ribbon if needs be.

5. Right-click on the page number or Click the Page Number command in the Headers & Footers ribbon to set the page numbers as desired.

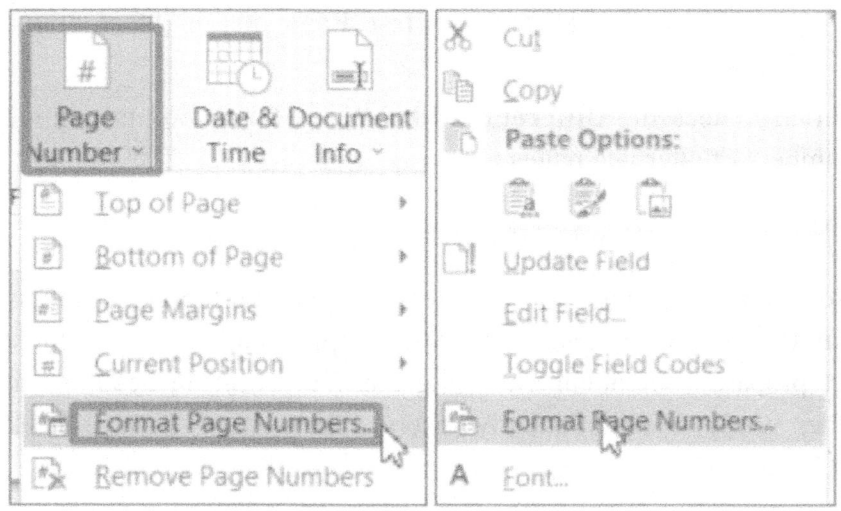

6. Continue **steps 3-5** above for all the sections as desired.

Removing Page Numbers.

To remove Page numbers from the entire document:

1. Go to the **Insert** ribbon.

2. Click **Page Number**.

A drop-down menu appears.

3. Select **Remove Page Number** from the options.

Alternatively,

1. Double-click on the Header or Footer area.

2. Select the page number and press the **Delete** key.

To remove the page number from the first page of the document or a section:

1. Double-click in the margin of the section or document to activate **Headers & Footers** Tools.

2. Check the **Different First Page** box in the Options group.

You can also check the **Different Odd & Even Pages** box to remove page numbers of alternate pages.

Inserting Automatic Table Of Content

Microsoft Word includes a tool that lets you create a table of contents either automatically or manually using simple templates. You must write or prepare your document using the Word built-in headings in the Styles group to automatically insert a table of contents. (Check **section 7.1.2** for how)

To Insert a Table of Contents:

1. Ensure your document headings uses Word built-in headings styles

2. Place your insertion point where you want the table of content to be.

3. Go to the **References** ribbon.

4. Click **Table of Contents**.

A drop-down menu appears.

5. Select an option:

• The first two options automatically insert your table of contents with **all** your available headings.

• The third option inserts the table of contents with placeholder texts and allows you to replace them with your own headings.

• Select **More Tables of Contents from Office.com** for more templates.

- Select the **Custom Table of Contents...** to customize your table. A dialog box appears, edit as desired, and press **OK**.

- If you already have a table of content in your document, you can delete it by selecting **Remove Table of Contents.**

Updating your Table of Contents

Word does not update your table of content automatically if you make changes to your document. You will have to update it manually.

To update your Table of Content:

1. Position your cursor in the table of content.

Table borders appear with buttons at the top-left.

2. Click the **Update Table** button.

A dialog box appears.

3. Click the **Update entire table**.

4. Press **OK**.

Word automatically updates your table.

Alternatively,

1. Right-click on the table of content.

A drop-down menu appears.

2. Select **Update Field.** You can also select **Update Table** in the **Table of Contents** group in the **References** ribbon.

A dialog box appears.

3. Click **Update the entire table**.

4. Click **OK**.

Note: Do not always forget to update your table after making significant changes that affect the headers or page numbers.

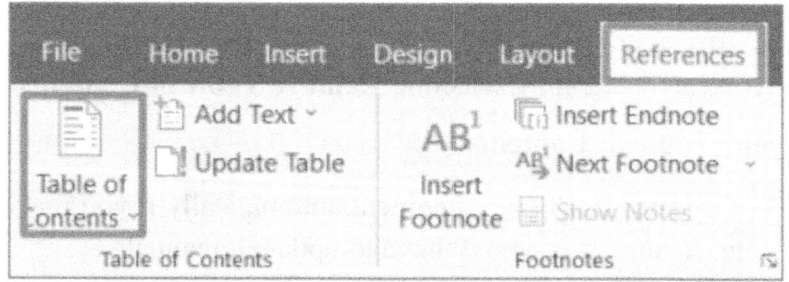

Adding Captions To Figures Or Objects

A caption is a title or brief explanation of a figure or an object mostly placed below a figure or an object to give information about the figure.

To add a caption to an object:

1. Select the object you want to add a caption to.

2. Go to the **References** tab.

3. Click **Insert Caption** in the **Captions** group.

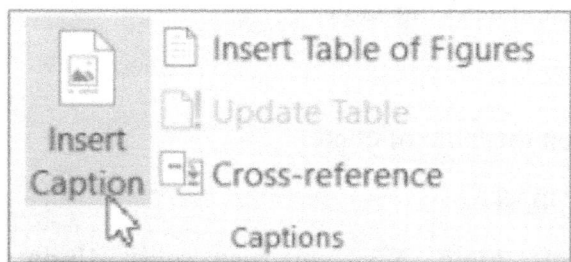

A caption dialog box appears.

4. Select **Figure** in the **Label** dropdown menu or any appropriate options.

5. Type the object description (it can include punctuations) in front of **Figure 1** in the **caption** text field.

6. Click **OK.**

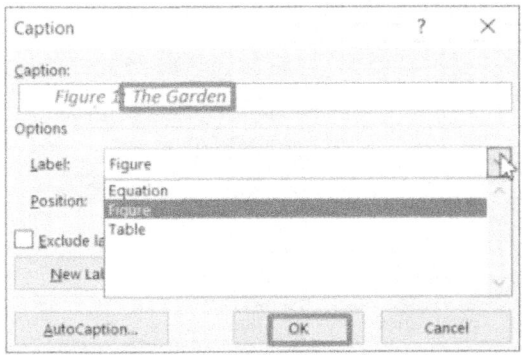

You can **format** your captions in the **Styles** group of the **Home** tab following the steps in **section 7.1**

To Add Chapter Number that updates automatically to your Image Caption.

1. Ensure you format your document headings with the Word **Headings** in the **Style** group. (Check **section 7.1** for more information).

2. Use the Word Multilevel list to number your chapter headings or **Heading 1** as the case may be following the steps below:

- Select any of your Chapters or Heading 1 style.

- Go to the **Home** tab.

- Click the **Multilevel List** icon in the **Paragraph** group.

- Select **Chapter 1 Heading…,** the last option, and all Headings 1 will be numbered automatically.

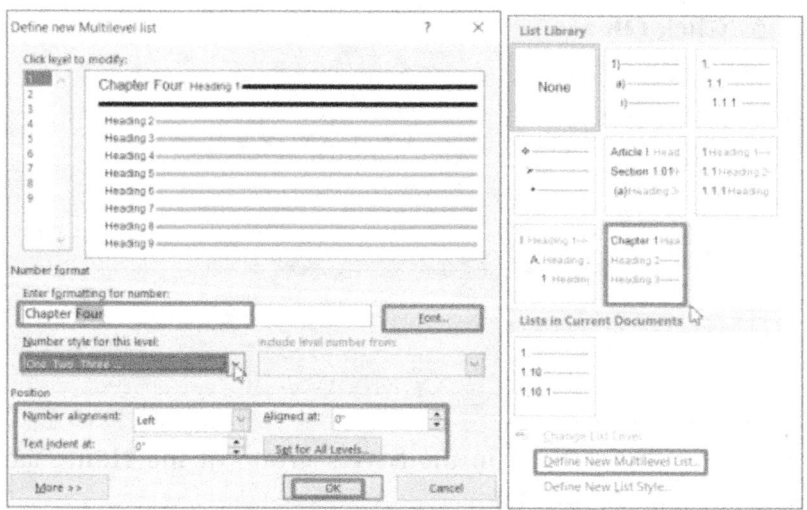

You can format the numbering in **Define new Multilevel** list. You can change the Chapter to a Section, change the numbers to words, change the font, and so on.

3. Select the object you want to add the caption.

4. Go to **References >> Captions >> Insert Caption**.

5. Select **Numbering** in the **Caption** dialog box.

A **Caption Numbering** dialog box appears.

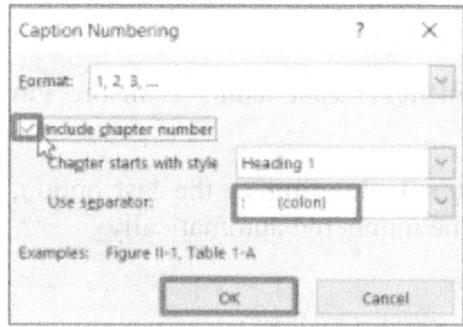

6. Check the **Include chapter number** box, select the desired separator, and press **OK**.

To make your captions sticks to your floating object:

1. Select the Object.

2. Go to the **Layout** tab.

3. Select **Wrap Text** command.

4. Choose any other options aside from the first from the dropdown list as desired. Alternatively, you can click on the Layout button at the top right corner of the object and select an option in the **With Text Wrapping** list.

5. Add a caption to your figure following the above steps.

6. Group the caption and the object (follow the steps in **section 5.11.3**)

To Delete a Caption: Select the caption and press Delete.

Note: Word automatically updates the figure numbers as you insert a new caption. You must update the caption or figure numbers whenever you delete or change the position of any caption.

To update the caption numbers:

1. Select all your document using **Ctrl + A.**

2. Right-click and select **Update Field** in the dialog box that appears **or**

Press **F9** to update the caption numbers.

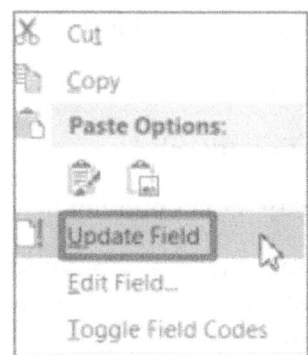

Inserting Automatic Table Of Figures

Word has a command to automatically add a table of figures to your work, just like adding a table of contents.

For you to automatically generate a table of figures, you must have added captions to all the figures used in your document using the Word **Insert Caption** command.

To Insert Table of Figures:

> 1. Ensure that you use the Word caption feature to add captions to your objects.
>
> 2. Place your insertion point where you want the table of figures to be.
>
> 3. Click the **References** tab.

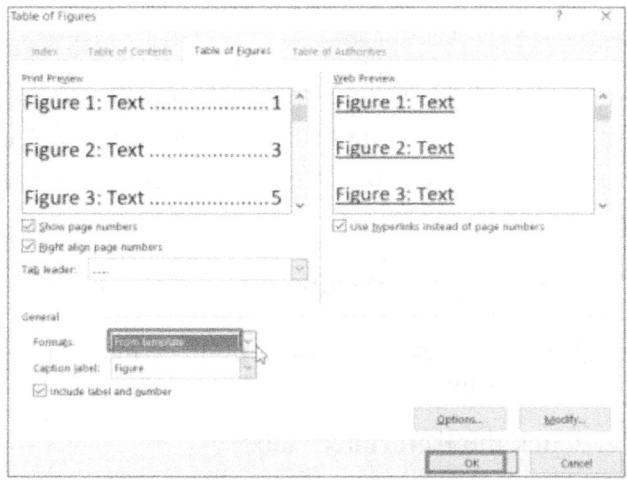

4. Select **Insert Table of Figures** in the **Caption** group. Table of Figures dialog box appears.

Select your desired Format, make other changes, preview, and press **OK**. Your table of figures appears in your document.

Inserting Cover Page

A cover page contains information about the document like the title, author, and other enticing objects or texts.

To insert a cover page:

1. Go to the **Insert** ribbon.

2. Click the **Cover Page** button in the **Pages** group.

A drop-down menu appears.

3. Select the desired templates to customize.

4. Edit, format, and the template to your taste. You can add images, text, and so on.

Working With Citations

Citation is a standard technique in academic writing that informs readers about the sources of quotes or paraphrases used in your text. To save you time and frustration, Word provides a tool that assists you with citations.

To insert Citation into your document:

1. Position your insertion point wherever you want to place your citation.

2. Click the **References** tab.

3. Click (Placeholder1) **Insert Citation** in the **Citations & Bibliography** group.

A drop menu appears.

4. Select **Add a New Source** option.

A dialog box appears.

5. Select the **Type of Source** (e.g., book, journal, article, etc.) using the dropdown arrow.

6. Fill in the source details in the text boxes provided.

7. Check the **Show All Bibliography Fields** for additional information.

8. Input the **Tag name**.

9. Press **OK,** and your citation is inserted.

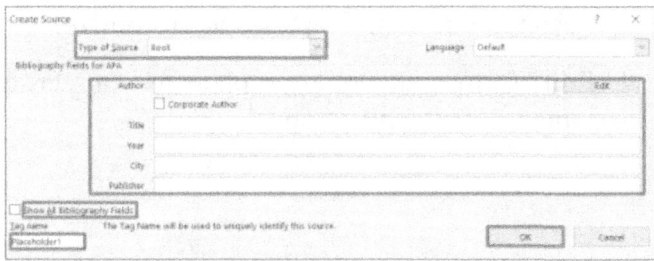

Inserting References, Works Cited, Or Bibliography

A bibliography is an alphabetical list of all sources you consulted for your document, whether or not you cited them. References and works cited are alphabetical lists of all the citations used in your document, whereas a bibliography is an alphabetical list of all sources you consulted for your document, whether or not This list is frequently seen towards the conclusion of a text.

The format style utilized distinguishes references from works cited. Different professional and academic groups use a variety of citation styles. When referencing works in APA (American Psychological Association) format, use references, and when citing works in MLA (Modern Language Association) format, use works cited list.

To insert References, Works Cited List, or Bibliography:

> 1. Ensure you use the Word **Citation** command to cite in your document body.
>
> 2. Place your insertion point wherever you want the lists to be.
>
> 3. Click the **References** tab.
>
> **4.** Click **Bibliography** in the **Citations & Bibliography** group.
>
> A drop-down menu appears.
>
> 5. Select an option, and it appears in your document.

Note: Any time you edit or add to the citations in your document, you must manually update your references, works cited, or bibliography. This can be done from the list or any of the citations in the document.

To Edit and update your citations:

- Select any of the citations in the document.

- Right-click on the citation or click the drop-down arrow.

- Select **Edit Source** from the menu that appears, edit the **Create source** dialog box, click **Ok,** and click **yes** to the prompt that appears.

- **To update**, click **Update Citations and Bibliography** instead**.**

or

- Select the references or bibliography.

- Click on the **Update Citations and Bibliography** button at the top left corner of the list border.

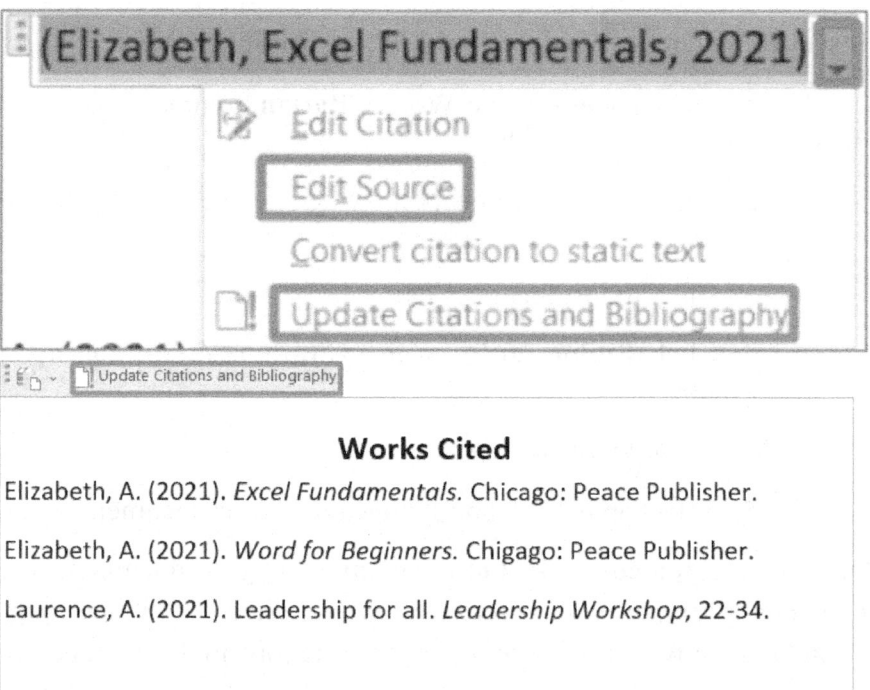

Works Cited

Elizabeth, A. (2021). *Excel Fundamentals.* Chicago: Peace Publisher.

Elizabeth, A. (2021). *Word for Beginners.* Chigago: Peace Publisher.

Laurence, A. (2021). Leadership for all. *Leadership Workshop,* 22-34.

Chapter 6.   Borders, Tables, Rows And Column

We'll learn how to build, insert, and remove borders, rows, and columns in this chapter. We'll also go through how to make a table of contents, a bullet and numbering list, an endnote, and footnotes in Microsoft Word, as well as the visuals.

Borders

A border is like a line coupled into a text, paragraph, or page of a document. This line can be in a different format, either thin or thick, single, double or triple, dashed, or with various art and color

Insert A Page Border In Microsoft Word 2024

Open a new or existing document on your computer. Then, on the Ribbon, select the Design tab. Then, on the page border, click. Scroll down to the borders and shading section. The dialogue box with the borders and shading appears. Select any type in the options section. box, 3D, shadow, and so on Click Apply to, which will enable you to select where you want it to appear on the document, and then click Ok. You can also change the color, style, art, and width of the border.

How To Add Border To A Part Of Text

Select the text you want to apply the border to. Click on the **page border** on the design tab and the dialogue box, click on any type and click Ok. The border will be added to that selected text in the document. Note you can also edit your border with the elements shown in the figure

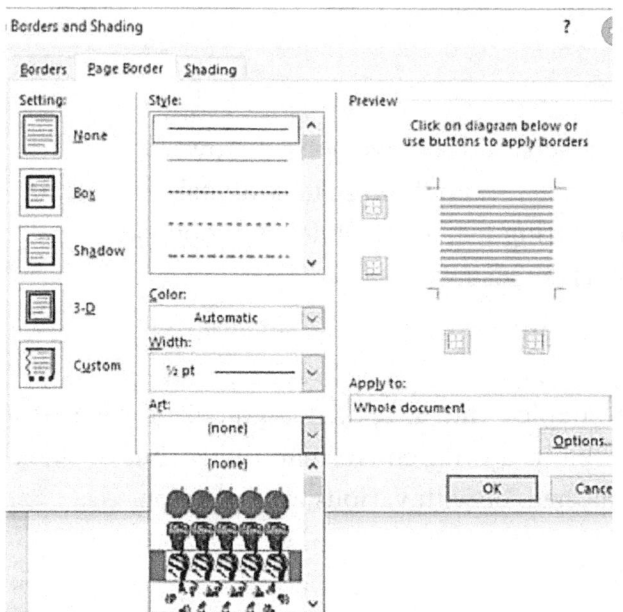

How To Add Border To A Paragraph

Select the paragraph. Click on the border on the design tab and click OK to apply a border to a paragraph.

To Remove A Border

Click on the None option on the dialogue box that pops up when you click on the page border button on the Design tab.

The Table On Microsoft Word 2024

How To Insert A Table

To begin, open a document on your computer. Place your cursor where you want the table to appear in the document. Select the table from the table group from the Insert tab. Move your cursor across and down to select the number of cells in your table that will be grouped as rows and columns. The selected cells will turn orange then click Insert table.

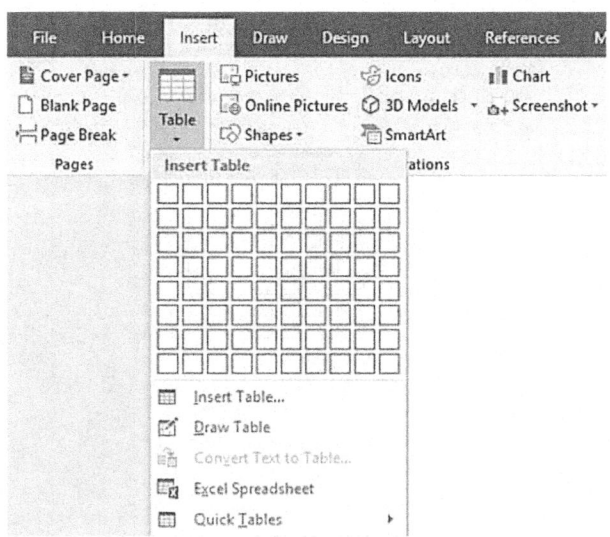

Quick Table

Quick tables are tables that you can change to suit your needs. To begin, place your cursor where you wish the table to be inserted. On the Ribbon, select the Insert tab. As indicated in the figure, select table from the table group, then fast table from the drop-down menu. From the gallery, select the table you desire. Then type over or delete the table example text to fill in your material.

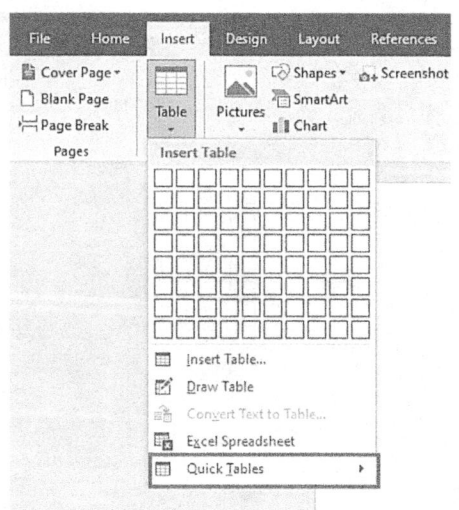

How Do I Enter Text Into A Table

To do this, place your cursor into a cell and type as you normally would enter a text into a table.

Table Styles

Click on the Design tab and then on Table Style, click on the drop-down button circled in the figure below, and different table styles show up then you can select any one of them.

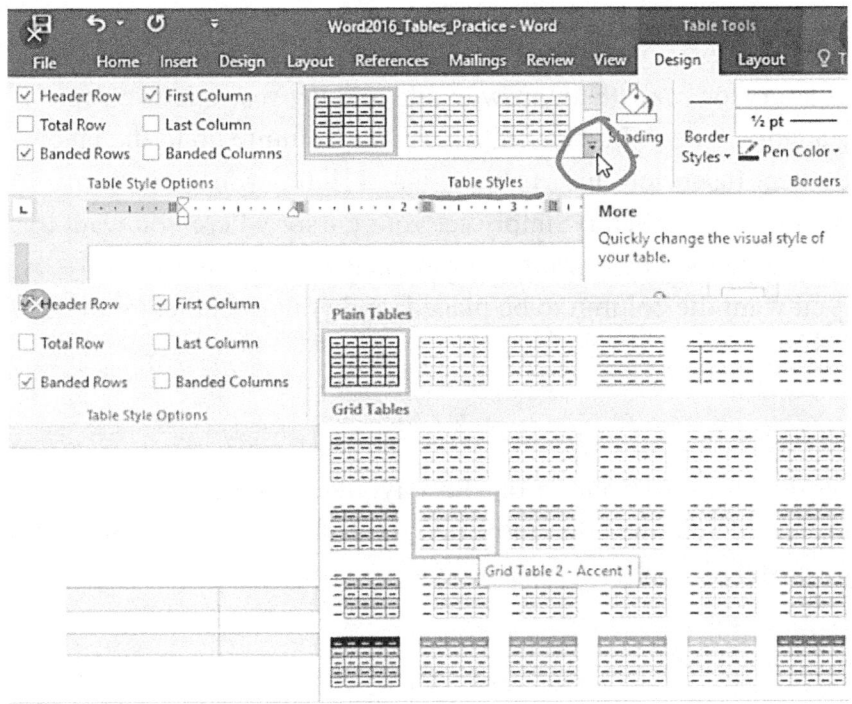

Note: You can use the shading menu to add a custom menu to individual rows and columns.

- **Header Row:** Only the header row is colored, the first row is highlighted

- **Banded Rows:** Alternate rows are highlighted

- **Total Row**: All rows are highlighted

- **First Column:** The first column is highlighted

- **Last Columns:** last columns are highlighted

- **Banded Column:** Alternate Column are highlighted

To Create Your Table Styles

Click on create new table style on the table style group and do lots of formatting on the dialogue box. Click okay when you're done.

Insert Rows And Column

Place your cursor beneath any row to add another row once you've created a table. Select the plus sign. To add a column, go to the layout tab and select Insert left, insert above, insert right, or insert bottom from the drop-down menu. Simply set your cursor where you want to add the column and click Insert column, then choose any location where you want the column to be placed, and your document will be modified.

Cut/Copy/Paste/Delete Rows And Columns

Click on the row and column on the Layout tab, you will see delete. Click on it to delete the column or just right-click with your mouse. It displays different options to cut, copy, paste or delete rows and column

Alternatively, to delete a table, select the table selector which is a + plus. It will select the entire table. Note that you may have to use the pointer over the table to reveal all the table selectors. Then right-click the table and select the delete table from the shortcut menu,

Resize Rows, Column, And Tables

Place your cursor in any column, then select the layout tab and cell size group. There is a height choice; click it to expand it, and the column's height will increase, as will the weight.

To make each column the same height, click distribute rows, and all rows will be the same height. To get an equal column, do the same thing with the column. Click on distribute column.

Click the resizing lever in the bottom right corner of the table to resize the entire table. To reveal the handle, you may need to slide your pointer over the table. Then, using the + sign on the table's bottom side, move the table to the desired size.

Split And Merge Cells

Select all the cells, click on the layout tab and click on merge cells while on split cell place your cursor on the cell, click on split cell, a dialogue box shows up to type in how many rows and columns you want, type in the number and click OK. That cell will be split into the number of rows and columns you typed in.

To split an entire table, keep your cursor anywhere you want to split the table. Click on the split table and it will be split.

How To Convert Text To Table

Select your text first. Click the drop-down arrow on the table groupings under the Insert tab. To convert text to a table, scroll down. Select a text separation option from the dialogue box. This is how Word determines what should go into each column. Then press OK.

Placing A Column Break

You can break a column in Word just like you can break a page. Only multicolumn pages can have this column break. It is beneficial for the column's text to come to a halt somewhere on the page and then resume at the top of the next column.

To do this: Click to place the insertion pointer in your document which will be the start of the next column and click the **Layout** tab. Thereafter, click on the **break** button located on the **page setup group**. A menu appears to click on the column. The text immediately moves to the top of the next column.

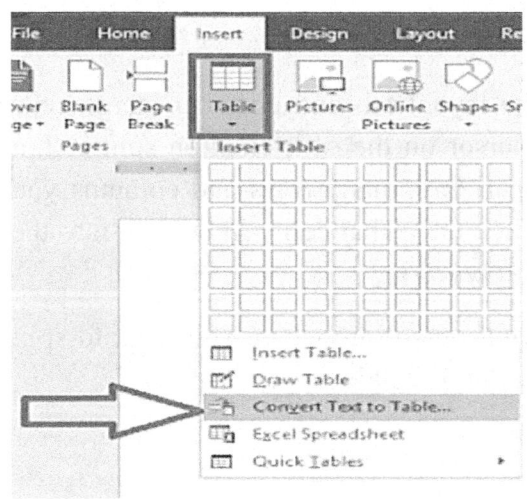

How To Create Bulleted List In Microsoft Word

When constructing a list that stands out from the text, bullet lists come in handy. To make a list using bullets. Place your cursor where you wish the bullet list to appear.

Go to the **home** tab, and on the **paragraph group,** click on the bullet, on the drop-down arrow, click on any bullet that suits you the best. Then type your first list item, after that, press enter and the second line start with the same bullet style. Double-click the enter key to end your bullet list.

To Remove The Bullet And Numbering

Just open the document and go to the home tab, click on the bullet icon and choose none.

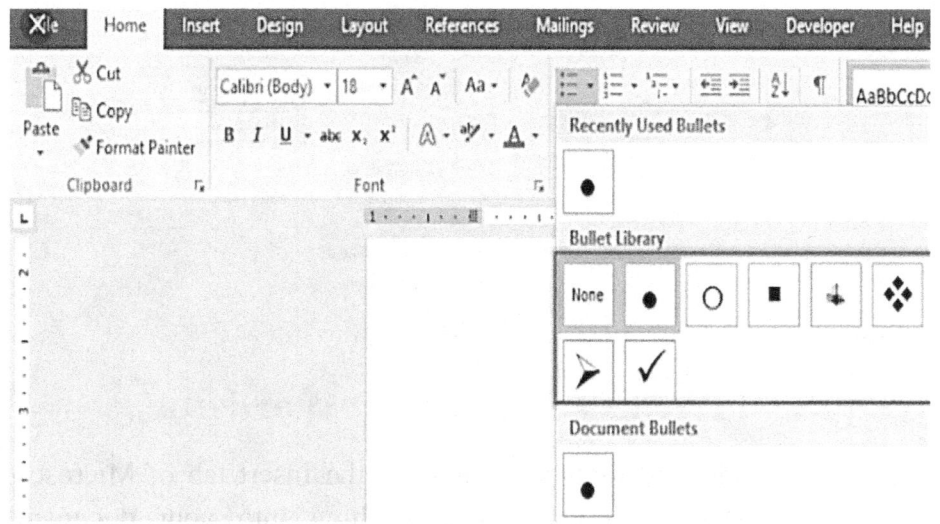

How To Insert Endnote And Footnote On Microsoft 2024

Footnotes are at the bottom of a page while **endnotes** are found at the end of a document. To begin, place your cursor where the superscript number for the footnote should appear. Select the **Reference tab** and select the dialogue box launcher in the footnote group. Select footnote or endnote from the drop-down menu, then select the note's intended location. Other options in the dialogue box, such as number formatting, should be explored. To build your footnote, select insert. After that, type your superscript number, and your cursor will shift to the new spot specified in the footnote and endnote dialogue boxes. Now type your note and double-click the number preceding it to return to the body content's matching superscript number. Insert the next note by placing your cursor where the superscript number for the next note should appear, then selecting Insert footnote or endnote from the footnote and endnote group.

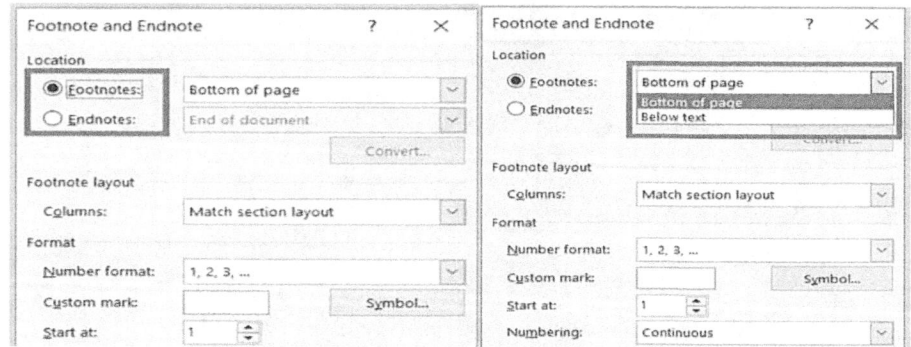

Graphical Works In Microsoft Word 2024

Most of the graphical tools are found on the Insert tab of Microsoft word 2024. Here, you can insert anything into your document including pictures, shapes, text, etc.

To Insert pictures: Place your cursor where you want the image to be inserted and click the Insert tab on the ribbon. The photo tool format tab is one of the commands. It will transport you to areas where you can insert different photos into your work when you click on it. When you've found the image you want, click Insert, and it'll be automatically updated in your document. Use one of the command buttons to select which type of image to add.

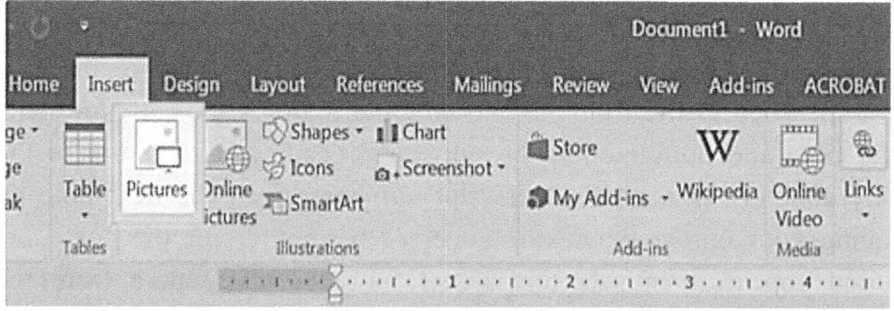

Note: You can also insert online pictures, by clicking on online pictures from the Insert tab. Then copy the image from the web and paste it into your document

- **To Delete an image,** click on the image, select it and click on the delete button.

- **To Copy and Paste an Image;** Select the image you want to copy from another document. Alternatively, press Ctrl + C to copy the image. Then go to the new location where you want to paste that image and click Ctrl + V to paste. Alternatively, right-click the mouse, and options are displayed, choose the paste option to paste the image

How To Insert Shape Into Your Document

You can Insert shapes into your document. Word has a section that contains some common shapes such as circles, squares, arrows, geometric figures, etc. To do this; Click Insert tab and click on the shape button. This menu has lots of shapes that you can choose from. Click on your preferred shape and it is updated into your document.

Note: you can adjust the shape in terms of size or colors. All you have to do is use the drawing tool format tab. This can be seen on the Ribbon. Just select the shapes to effect those changes. You can use the **Shape Fill button t**o set the fill color and you can use the Shape Outline button to set the shape's outline color. You can also adjust the outline thickness (Shape outline button menu) weight and effect (3D, shadow, or any fancy formatting)on the selected shape.

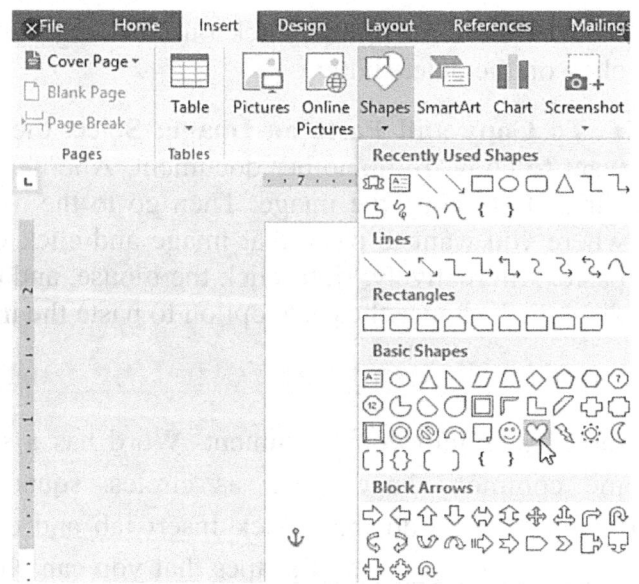

How To Create Picture Layout On Microsoft Word 2024

First of all, select the picture and a new box appears on the selected picture. On the **picture style group,** there is an option for a **picture layout**. Click on it and then a list of different Layout will be displayed. Click on the one that suits you and resize to the box.

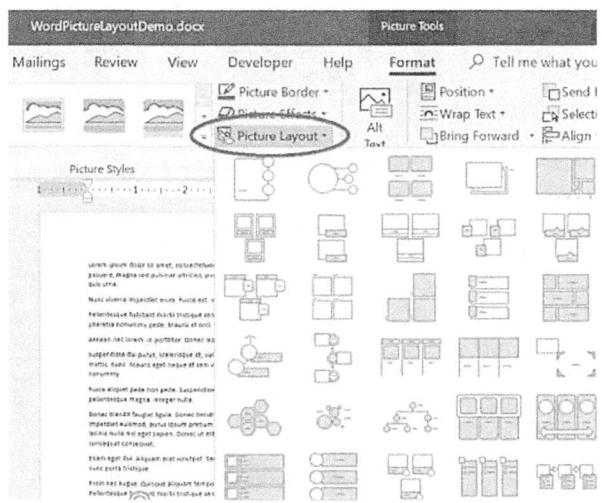

How To Wrap Text Around An Image

It is important to provide a proper layout option to keep all text and images in your document well organized. This layout has 3 general groups. The **Inline** (where the image is inserted into the text and the image acts as a character), **wrapped** (text stays around the image), and **floating** (where the image is seen at the front or behind the text).

To enter an image layout, first select an image, then click the Layout Options button, which displays a list of possible layout options. Inline, square, tight, through, behind the text, top and bottom, front if text, behind the text, wrap text, and so on are some of the alternatives. Click on more selections to see more choices. Choose your favorite option and click OK.

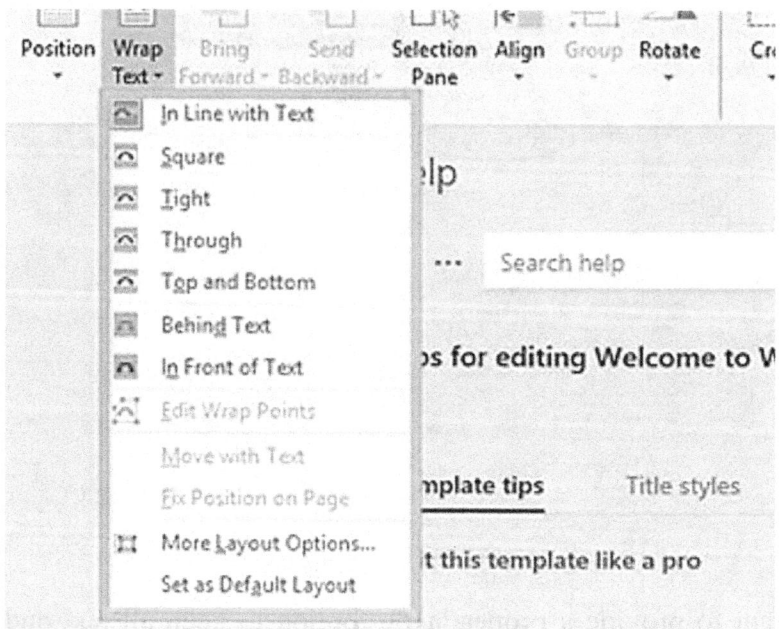

How To Resize An Image

When you click to select an image, eight corner handles display as dots around the image. This is how you scale an image to make it bigger or smaller. To rotate the image, use the top long handle circled on the image with the rotate icon.

How To Crop An Image

To crop an image, click to select the image and on the picture formatting tool in the size group, there is the crop button. Click on the button and press the enter to cut out any part of the image.

As a way of conclusion, all images can be edited to suit your choice. You can choose to rotate or change the position of the image. This can be achieved with the picture formatting tool.

Chapter 7.   Managing Documents and Word Windows

Saving Your Document

After you've finished producing your document, save it for later use or sharing.

Your document can be saved to your computer, a disk drive, a CD drive, a USB device, or OneDrive. When you save your work in OneDrive, you may access it from any computer that has access to your account.

To save your document for the first time:

   1. Click on the **File** tab to go to the backstage of Word.

   2. Click **Save As** option in the left-side panel.

   3. Select where you want to save your document in the right-side pane.

A dialog box appears.

   4. Change the document name to your desired name in the **File Name** box.

   5. Select the format in which you want to save your document in the **Save as type** dropdown list.

   6. Click **Save**.

You will have to save your work anytime you make changes.

To save your document subsequently,

   1. Click on the **Save** icon 🖫 in the quick access toolbar or **Save** tab in the backstage view.

Alternatively,

2. use the shortcut key **Ctrl + s.**

Note: Using the above methods for the document that has never been saved will initiate the **Save as** command.

Your already saved document can also be duplicated with the same or different name and in the same or different location by selecting the **Save As** option in the Word backstage.

Page Setups For Printing

You can get a hard or paper copy of your document by printing.

To print your document:

1. Ensure your computer is connected to the printer.

2. Ensure your printer is loaded with the right size papers.

3. Click the **File** tab to go to the Word backstage.

4. Select **Print** in the left side pane.

Print pane appears by the right-side.

5. Input the number of copies you want directly or with the arrows in the **Copies** box.

6. Select a printer in the **Printer** drop-down if your computer is connected to more than one printer.

7. Under **Settings**, the default settings are shown in each box. To make changes to any, click the drop-down in front of the one you want to change and select your preferred option in the drop-down menu.

• You can print specified page numbers by inputting them in the **Pages** textbox, separated by a comma.

• The paper orientation, page size, and margins appear as you have set them during formatting. You could adjust them here if you desired.

- Click on the **Page Setup** for more page settings.

8. Preview your work in the right section of the **Print** pane to see how it will come out. Make use of the scroll bar to go through the pages.

9. Click the **Print** button.

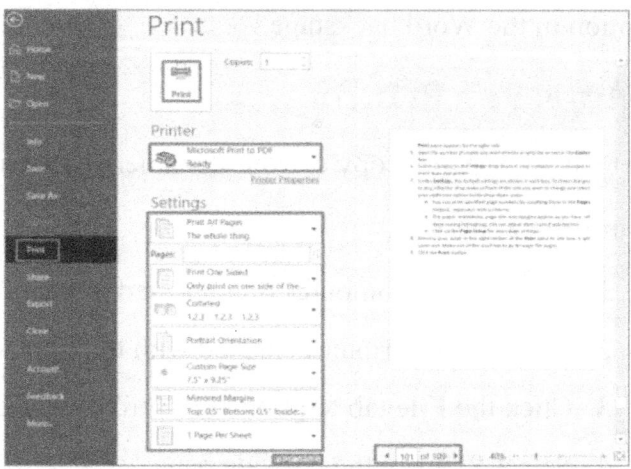

Sharing Document By Email

Your word document can be easily shared directly as an email body or as an attachment to an email address with the **Send to Mail Recipient** command in Word. **Send to Mail Recipient** command is not available in the Word user interface by default and needs to be added. You can preferably add it to the Quick Access Toolbar by customizing it.

To add 'Send to Mail Recipient' to Quick Access Toolbar (QAT):

1. Right-click on the **QAT**.

A dialog box appears.

2. Select **Customize Quick Access Toolbar**.

Word Options dialog box appears.

3. From the **Choose commands from** drop-down list, choose **Commands Not in the Ribbon**.

4. Locate **Send to Mail Recipient** in the list. The list is arranged alphabetically for easy location.

5. Click **Add>>** button.

Word adds it to Customize Quick Access Toolbar.

6. Click **OK,**

and it appears in your Quick Access Toolbar.

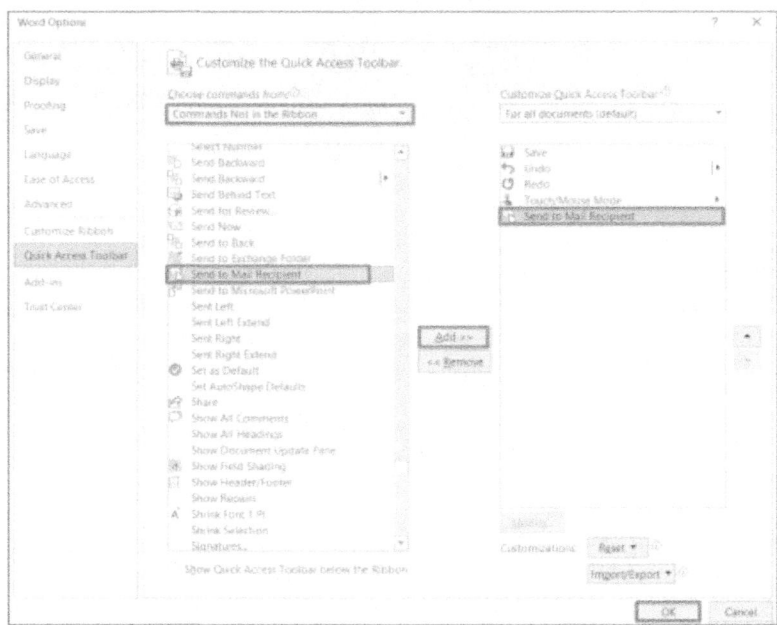

To share your document as an email body:

1. Ensure your computer is connected and sign in to your email account.

2. Click on **Send to Mail Recipient** command in the Quick Access Toolbar.

The mail Composing window appears under the ribbon with your document title already added.

3. Add the recipient's email address and other information as desired. You can also change the title as desired.

4. Ensure you have an internet connection.

5. Click **Send a Copy**.

Word sends your document and closes the composing email window. To close the email window manually, click on the icon in the Quick Access Toolbar.

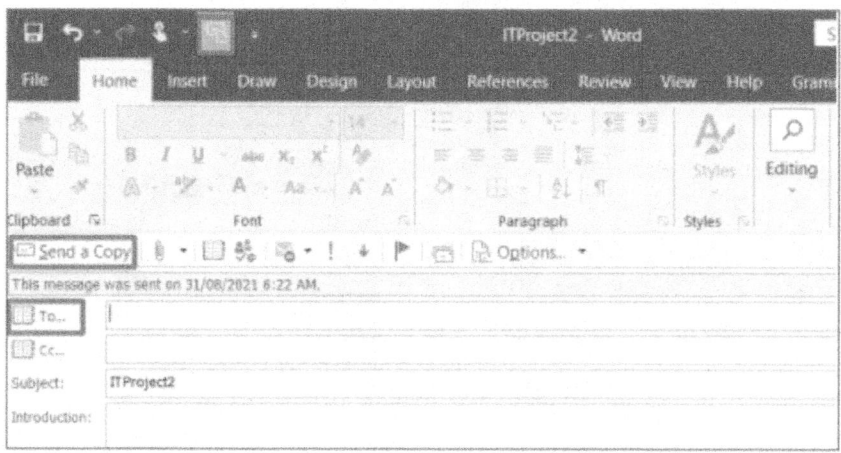

Protecting Your File With Word Security Features

After you've spent time and effort generating your document, you'll need to safeguard it against plagiarism, stealing, inadvertent alteration, and a variety of other security issues.

Word has incredible security capabilities that can help you secure your document depending on how critical it is.

To secure your word document:

1. Go to the Word Backstage by clicking the **File** tab.

2. Click the **Info** tab in the left side pane.

Info pane appears on the right side.

3. Click the **Protect Document** button.

A dialog box appears.

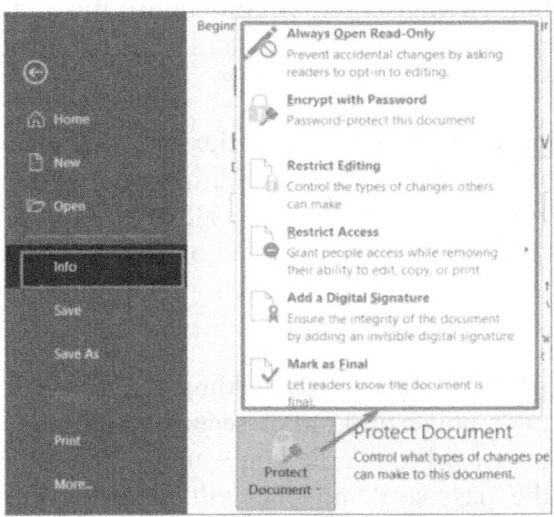

4. Select an option from the list.

• **Mark as Final:** This makes your document read-only (i.e., typing, editing, and proofing capabilities disabled) with a message at the top of the document screen informing the reader that the document is final. However, any reader can still edit and resave the document by clicking the **Edit Anyway** button in the top message. Select this security feature only if you just need to notify the reader that it is the recommended final version of your document or to discourage editing.

• **Add a Digital Signature:** Protecting your document with a digital signature has several benefits, like maintaining proof of document integrity, signer identity, and others. You must purchase a digital signature from a

91

verified Microsoft partner to use it. Selecting this option for the first time will prompt you to where you can get one.

- **Restrict Access:** This allows others to view your document but prevents them from copying, modifying, sharing, or printing it. To help safeguard the document, you'll need to connect to the Information Right Management (IRM) server. If you choose this option, you will be prompted to connect and guided through the procedure.

- **Restrict Editing:** This is a flexible way of securing your document from anyhow editing and gives control over the type of editing that the allowed people can do. Selecting this option opens a pane on the right side of the document to set formatting restrictions, editing restrictions, and **start enforcement**.

- **Encrypt with Password:** Adding a password to your document is a powerful kind of security, and you can only offer the password to people you want to have access to it. Without the password, no one will be able to open, let alone change, your document. When you choose this option, Word will prompt you to enter a password and confirm it.

- **Always Open Read-Only:** This feature prevents your document from accidental editing by always opening it as read-only. A dialog box appears each time you want to open it, notifying you that the document will be opened as read-only. Press **Yes** to continue and **No** if there is a need to make changes.

5. Follow all the prompts based on your choice and press ok.

6. Close your document for the security setting to take effect.

Closing Your Word Document

To close your document after you are done:

- Click the **X** button at the top-right corner of the Word window.

Or

- Go to the **File** tab and select the **Close** option in the left-side pane.

Or

- Use the shortcuts keys, **Ctrl + F4** or **Ctrl + W.**

Microsoft word closes or notifies you if you try to close your document without saving it.

Recovering Unsaved Document

It can happen that you mistakenly close your document without saving your last changes. The good news is that Word has an **autosave** feature that allows you to recover your file with the last unsaved changes.

To recover your unsaved documents:

1. Go to the backstage view by clicking on the **File** tab.

2. Click the **Open** tab.

Open pane appears.

3. Click the **Recover Unsaved Documents** button at the bottom of the recently opened document list.

The location dialog box appears with the list of unsaved documents.

4. Select the likely document. You can check the date to know the likely document.

5. Click the **Open** button.

The document opens.

6. Save the document accordingly.

Alternatively,

1. Go to the backstage view by clicking on the **File** tab.

2. Click the **Info** tab.

Info pane opens.

3. Select **Manage Document** dropdown.

4. Click the **Recover Unsaved Documents** menu that appears.

The location dialog box appears with the list of unsaved documents.

5. Follow **steps 4-6** above.

Opening Saved Document

You can open your document from the Word application or directly from your device.

To open an existing document from Word:

1. Go to the backstage view by clicking on the **File** tab.

2. Click the **Open** tab.

Open pane appears.

3. Select the location of your document.

Open dialog box appears.

4. Select the folder or your document. You can scroll down the left side list of locations on your device to locate your document.

5. Click **Open**.

Alternatively, if you recently opened your document or pinned it to Word, it will be available in the **Recent** or **Pinned** list in the backstage **Home** panel, and you can click on it to open it.

If you often use or work on your document, it will be better to pin it in Word.

To pin your document to word:

1. Locate the document in the recent list.

2. Move your cursor over the document.

3. Click the pin icon in front of the file.

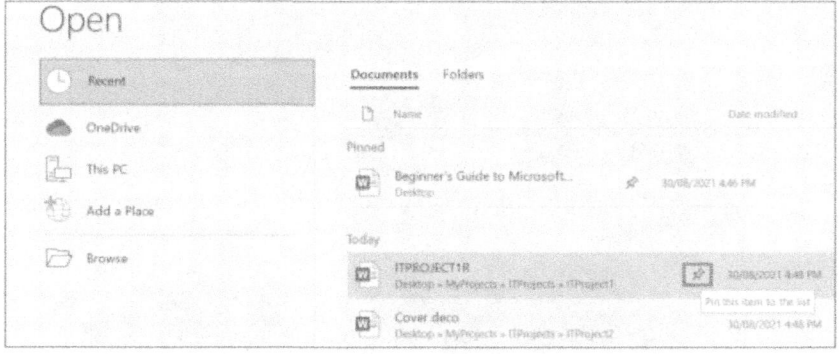

To open an existing document from your device:

1. Ensure you have the Word application installed on your computer.

2. Locate your Word document on your device.

3. Double-click to open it if it has a Word icon, if not, right-click on the file.

Select **open with** from the menu that appears and select **Word**.

Chapter 8. Word   Top   Shorcut Commands

Working with Keyboard shortcut commands can reduce your stress, save your time and increase your productivity to a considerable extent. Below are the top shortcut commands you can use to work smartly in Word.

SN	Shortcuts	Functions
1.	Ctrl + A	4. To select all the content of your document
2.	Ctrl + B	5. To bold the highlighted contents
3.	Ctrl + C	6. To copy highlighted text
4.	Ctrl + D	7. To open a Font dialog box
5.	Ctrl + E	8. To center align the selected content
6.	Ctrl + F	9. To open the **Find Navigation** pane
7.	Ctrl + G	10. To open the **Go To** dialogue window
8.	Ctrl + H	To open the **Replace** dialog box.
9.	Ctrl + I	11. To italicize highlighted contents
10.	Ctrl + J	12. To justify align selected content
11.	Ctrl + K	13. To open the **Insert Hyperlink** dialog box.
12.	Ctrl + L	14. To left-align selected content

13.	**Ctrl + M**	15. To increase the Indent
14.	**Ctrl + N**	To create a new blank document
15.	**Ctrl + O**	To open an already saved document
16.	**Ctrl + P**	To go to **the Print** tab in the backstage view
17.	**Ctrl + Q**	To reset selected paragraph
18.	**Ctrl + R**	To right-align selected content
19.	**Ctrl + S**	To save your current document
20.	**Ctrl + T**	To increase the Hanging indent of the selected paragraph.
21.	**Ctrl + U**	To underline the selected text.
22.	**Ctrl + V**	To paste what you copied last.
23.	**Ctrl + W**	To close your document
24.	**Ctrl + X**	To cut selected content
25.	**Ctrl + Y**	To redo the last action, you undo.
26.	**Ctrl + Z**	To undo your last action
27.	**Shift +Ctrl +A**	To apply the All caps command
28.	**Shift +Ctrl +C**	To copy Format
29.	**Shift +Ctrl +D**	To double underline selected text
30.	**Shift +Ctrl +G**	To open the Word count dialog box
31.	**Shift +Ctrl +J**	To distribute the letters of the

		selected text evenly
32.	**Shift +Ctrl +K**	To apply the Small-cap command
33.	**Shift +Ctrl +L**	To apply bullet listing.
34.	**Shift +Ctrl +M**	To decrease Indent
35.	**Shift +Ctrl +N**	To apply Normal Style of the **Style** group.
36.	**Shift +Ctrl +O**	To open the research pane
37.	**Shift +Ctrl +P**	To open the Font dialog box
38.	**Shift +Ctrl +Q**	To set the Font to symbol.
39.	**Shift +Ctrl +T**	To decrease Hanging Indent.
40.	**Shift +Ctrl +V**	To open the Paste Format window.
41.	**Shift +Ctrl +W**	To underline each word of the selected content.
42.	**Esc**	To cancel an active command
43.	**F1**	To open Microsoft Word **Help**
44.	**Ctrl + Alt + V**	To display the **Paste Special** dialog box
45.	**Ctrl + Shift + F**	To open the Fonts tab of the **Format Cells** dialog box.

Chapter 9. Conclusion

Personal information is created, edited, formatted, saved, stored, and even printed using word processing.

Individuals and businesses alike utilize Microsoft Word, the most extensively used word-processing application tool. It comes with all of the tools you'll need to solve all of your document development issues. These tools are simple to use and save a significant amount of time.

Microsoft Word is a fantastic program that can be used by students, instructors, and business executives. It comes with a number of built-in templates that you can use to create and personalize visually appealing documents that are simple to edit, share, and print.

With the chapters covered above. We can conclude that;

- Microsoft Word is a very useful word-processing tool.
- Its benefits cut across personal and professional assignments.
- It is faster and easier to use than writing by hand.
- It has a lot of formatting choices and styles.
- Documents created can be stored in your computer or any other memory and can be shared.

Your document can be printed as a hard copy.

Thank you for reading this book.